# DRESSING THE MAN YOU LOVE

*A Woman's Guide
to Purchasing, Coordinating, and Caring
for His Classic Wardrobe*

Betsy Durkin Matthes

**Peter's
Pride
Publishing**
Shelter Island, New York
First Edition

Published by

**Peter's
Pride
Publishing**

Post Office Box 3026
Shelter Island, New York 11965-3026
PetersPridePub@optonline.net
http://PetersPridePublishing.com

Copyright @ 2006, by Betsy Durkin Matthes
Printed in 2006
Library of Congress Control Number:  2005909791
Matthes, Betsy Durkin
Dressing The Man You Love: A Woman's Guide to Purchasing, Coordinating, and Caring for His Classic Wardrobe/ Betsy Durkin Matthes - 1st ed.
Includes bibliography references, index, and glossary.
ISBN 0-9773878-3-6
1. Men's clothing   2. Grooming for Men   3. Title
Book design and production: Tracy Turner with Chris Spooner
Cover artwork: ©Erika Oller, Courtesy MHS Licensing
Illustrations: Daniel Cooney
Author's photo: Peter Charlton Matthes

Printed in the United States of America

This book is dedicated to
my father Robert, my husband Jack, my son Peter
and to

## Leslie Ellen

my loving friend who believed in
its importance from the very first word,
and who lost her battle with cancer
before it could be completed

# Acknowledgments

To Geraldine Kazenoff who first asked me the question. "What would you like to do that you have never done?" And so the adventure of this book began.

To Joan Jaffe, actress, comedian, and dearest friend, who first inspired me with her "successful image" classes at the Screen Actors Guide, to seriously research men's classic attire.

To Candace Whitman my copy/content editor and indexer, an author and illustrator of numerous children's books. How was I ever lucky enough to find you?

To Erika Oller my cover artist who honored me with the magic of her loveable characters.

To Tracy Turner my talented book designer and trusted confident through all the years of raising our sons at The Allen-Stevenson School, including a special thanks to patient and hardworking, Chris Spooner.

To Daniel Cooney who graced the text with his delightful and, oh so helpful illustrations.

To my proofreader Vincent Torre who enlightened me from the margins with his "male perspective".

To Hank and Dean Vogel who allowed me to experience their joy in creating the perfect men's shoe.

To Bob and Kate Ermillio whose three generations of tailoring know-how they so generously confided.

To Deb Venman of Beau Ties Ltd., Gustavo Taveras and Gary Babyatzky of Paron Fabrics, Todd Kelly of Mood Inc., Anthony Lilly of B&J Fabrics, Nicole Semhon-Kabbaz of American Sember Trading Corporation, Carol J. Konop of The Shirt Store and Joseph Salsedo of Whaler's Cleaners.

And to the many women who have shared with me their positive experiences with dressing beloved fathers, sons, husbands, and boyfriends, including Elizabeth Baxter, Maggie Davis, Alice Dreier, Mollie Fennell, Jody Thompson, Susan McMullen, Regina Robinson, Jo-Ann Robotti, and Caroline Temerian.

# The "Before You Read This Book" Quiz

In order to help you to better evaluate your knowledge of men's attire, I have prepared a true and false quiz (minus any and all demands for a perfect performance!). The intention of this quiz is to give you an idea of where you presently stand. I encourage you, likewise, to come back when you have read the book and take the test again. This should give you a fuller assessment of all that you have learned and, along with it, the secret pleasure of knowing just how much of an expert you have really become.

1   Men shopping with women will get more attention     T     F
    from salespeople.

2   Knowing your most flattering colors can be very helpful     T     F
    in selecting colors for him.

3   The evening news anchor can tell you a lot about what     T     F
    the well-dressed man is wearing.

4   One of the most popular and safest combinations for men     T     F
    is a navy blue suit, white dress shirt, and a red tie.

5   A tall man should select suits and jackets that are made     T     F
    up in larger patterns.

6   If he can only afford to buy two business suits, the second     T     F
    should be a dark brown.

7   If the pockets of a suit are basted shut when purchased,     T     F
    the stitches should be gently removed before wearing.

8   A pastel dress shirt is totally out of place in an     T     F
    office environment.

| | | | |
|---|---|---|---|
| 9 | A short man will look best in a tie that is narrow. | T | F |
| 10 | Gabardine ironed at too high a heat will retain a permanent shine. | T | F |
| 11 | Suspenders and a belt are never worn at the same time. | T | F |
| 12 | "The rise" is the amount of room in a man's trousers located between the waistband and the bottom of the crotch. | T | F |
| 13 | A heavy-set man should never consider wearing a double-breasted jacket. | T | F |
| 14 | "Casual Fridays" are a time when a man can totally enjoy being comfortable without concern for office dress codes. | T | F |
| 15 | When an invitation states "Black Tie Only," a navy blue or black suit with a white shirt and dark tie is considered acceptable attire. | T | F |
| 16 | Etiquette requires that you work with the first sales-person who approaches you on the sales floor. | T | F |
| 17 | Trousers with pleats are considered to be dressier than those without. | T | F |
| 18 | Hand-stitching is the most obvious sign of an inferior-quality garment. | T | F |
| 19 | One of the easiest alterations for a tailor is the shortening or lengthening of a jacket. | T | F |
| 20 | Any plain, black oxford can be considered as a dress shoe. | T | F |
| 21 | A dress-shirt cuff should always extend beyond his business suit sleeve by ⅛ of an inch. | T | F |

22  His belt size corresponds directly to the size found on the    T    F
    waist of his trousers.

23  With checked shirts, the smaller the pattern, the dressier    T    F
    the shirt is perceived to be.

24  If the stain on a tie is water-based, rubbing it immediately    T    F
    with a wet napkin will normally take the stain right out.

25  Suspenders only come in one size.    T    F

26  Because socks are universally sized, he need not concern    T    F
    himself with their country of origin.

27  A pocket square can be a delightful accent to a man's attire    T    F
    and can also be handy on occasion for blowing his nose.

28  A shirt that has been heavily starched will shrink less, and    T    F
    will wear far longer.

29  In a well-made shoe, the front of the heel should rest solidly    T    F
    on a flat surface, while the back of the heel should not.

30  A tie can normally be washed in soap flakes if it is pushed    T    F
    back into shape afterward and placed on a clean towel to
    dry slowly overnight.

# How did you do?

| | | | | | |
|---|---|---|---|---|---|
| 1- | True | 11- | True | 21- | False |
| 2- | False | 12- | True | 22- | False |
| 3- | True | 13- | False | 23- | True |
| 4- | True | 14- | False | 24- | False |
| 5- | True | 15- | False | 25- | False |
| 6- | False | 16- | False | 26- | True |
| 7- | False | 17- | True | 27- | False |
| 8- | False | 18- | False | 28- | False |
| 9- | True | 19- | False | 29- | True |
| 10- | True | 20- | True | 30- | False |

If you scored 28 correct answers or more on this quiz, you are well equipped to take on the job of helping your man improve his wardrobe. This book will then prove most helpful to you in refining and clarifying any lingering confusion about the correct selections for him.

If you scored 26 to 23 you have some basic knowledge about men's clothing. This book will help you fill in any gaps and allow you to develop some expertise.

If you scored below 22, never mind. This book will assist you in learning very important entry-level knowledge, from which you can move on to cover more advanced information as well.

In any event, I encourage you to read other more specialized books on various areas of men's attire as interests you–topics such as the history of men's ties, the construction of men's shoes, and the art of custom tailoring. (See bibliography at the back of this book.)

*"Knowledge is of two kinds. We know a subject ourselves, or we know where we can find information upon it."*

*Samuel Johnson*

# Contents

Going Solo
His Time, This Time
Anytime Is Not the Right Time for Shopping
Never a Moody Man

## III THE CONSUMMATE MENSWEAR CONSUMER

That Personal Touch
Playing Your Part
Your Power As a Woman
A Keeper
A Loser
Shopping Royalty
The Value of a Good Salesperson

Suiting Himself
The British Silhouette
The Updated British/Ivy League
The Ivy League "Sack Suit"
The Continental Look
Size Does Count
Single-Breasted/Double-Breasted
Getting a Hold of His Lapels
Pick a Pocket
Vents (Single & Double)
Suit Buttons
Recognizing Quality

Wool
Woolens and Worsted
How Wool Is Graded
Wools Used in Men's Suits–A List

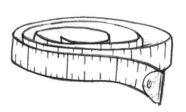

Special Consideration
Creating the Fail-Proof Roadmap

# Why I Wrote This Book

Some years ago, through my family I had occasion to meet and become friendly with a man named Charles. Charles was employed by Kilgour French & Stanbury the world- famous shop for men's custom-wear clothing that is located in London's Savile Row, the legendary street where princes and heads of state routinely have selected their attire since 1882.

My friend Charles would travel to New York twice each year, settling himself in an elegant but understated hotel in mid-Manhattan not far from the Plaza. There he would set out his endless array of designs and fabrics for custom-made suits, jackets, and outerwear. Every day, all day, he would take careful measurements from his newly-acquired patrons, as well as execute follow-up fittings for previously ordered garments from members of his well-established clientele.

Charles was the most beautifully dressed man I have ever known. It was a joy to meet him for a quick lunch or dinner just for the pleasure of gazing upon another one of his exquisite outfits. Ever since that time, I have appreciated and admired a well-dressed man. Any woman who thinks that men's fashion is nothing short of boring has never met Charles.

# Introduction

*"Clothes make the man. Naked people have little or no influence on society."*

Mark Twain

By and large we women enjoy clothes shopping.

Men do not.

We find it a pleasurable experience, a sort of treasure hunt away from the normal stresses of our everyday lives.

*"Whoever said money can't buy happiness simply didn't know where to go shopping."*

Bo Derek

Men shop when they must, and usually at the last minute.

When we women are successful in purchasing that perfect something which is going to make us look more attractive and feel more confident no matter what the social situation, we get a warm fuzzy feeling all over.

Men have feelings too, but not of the warm fuzzy "shopping" variety.

It is totally understandable that men who feel confused about where and when and what to buy, will hate shopping. For that reason men have always turned to the trusted women in their lives to provide them with the answers.

The way a man dresses is a statement to the world: "This is who I am." Although it often seems to a woman that a man's opportunities for self-expression through his clothing choices are severely limited, this is not the case at all. Possibilities for personal expression are as high and as wide as his imagination–and yours–will take him.

Because we women are often the hostesses of the gatherings we attend, we are well aware that the care each guest takes in dressing is always a strong indication of how important he or she considers a particular occasion.

Fashion can be frivolous. Like the changing lengths of women's skirts, what's "in" for men can be counted on to waffle from one shallow extreme to the other as one fashion season follows another. Men who chase after the latest fashion flavor wind up with a closet full of out-of-date, seldom used discards, perhaps even weighted down by the burden of overextended credit cards.

*"Fashions fade, style is eternal."*

*Yves Saint Laurent*

In agreeing to take on the job of helping your man to choose a totally new wardrobe, or to skillfully revive a prehistoric one, you have taken on a serious challenge. Gone are the days when a wrong choice was little more than a blip in his clothing allotment. One trip to a good quality men's shop will leave you both with a major attack of price tag anxiety.

The purpose of this book is to push you through the door marked "men only" and to enable you, the loved and trusted companion, to explore for yourself the fascinating world of men's fashion. It is designed to educate you to recognize superb craftsmanship by a highly respected tailor, understand the soft and sensual feel of a buttery worsted, and master the art of skillfully combining color, pattern and texture in a rich, yet subtle, ensemble. You will possess the knowledge to use to full advantage your man's best physical attributes and individual personality traits. You will be able to select the best of whatever you are looking for at prices that you can afford, choosing timeless styles that will wear well for many years to come.

And you will also be letting that very special man in your life know how much he really means to you.

*"The definition of a beautiful woman is one who loves me."*

*Sloan Wilson*

# How to Use This Book

## I Getting to Know Him

I begin by helping you to evaluate the right clothing choices for your man based on his height, his weight and his unique coloring. Basic rules of proportion are discussed using a wide range of body types. His best colors and color contrasts are also discussed. Armed with specific knowledge regarding his most attractive looks, you will be ready to move on to the next section.

## II Proper Prior Planning

This section sets the stage for your foray into the inner sanctum of his bedroom closet. This is the moment for discarding those things which simply no longer measure up. Included here are recommendations of things you will want to do on your own in order to get yourself comfortable in the world of men's apparel.

## III The Consummate Menswear Consumer

This section introduces you to the act of shopping for men's clothing. You will learn how to work well with sales staff and in-house tailors, how to evaluate what is well made and what isn't, how to mix and match patterns and textures, and how to properly accessorize for both casual and formal occasions.

## IV Preserving His Newly-Acquired Assets

Having invested in a classic wardrobe of finely-made clothing, this section will aid you in increasing the longevity of his newly-acquired treasures. Best-of-care suggestions are included for suits, trousers, coats, sweaters, shirts, shoes, as well as tips for proper pressing, cleaning, mending, polishing, laundering and storage.

## V The Launching of the New Him

Any positive change in our lives takes time to assimilate. Fear of making a mistake holds us back from the ability to forge ahead. Your man is no different. For this reason the final section provides a plan, which when initiated by you, will provide him with the information he needs to select each day's attire easily and with complete assurance. Future compliments from family and friends will build his confidence, while gradually enabling him to more fully trust his own instincts.

*Getting to know him*

1

# The Perfect
# (and Not So Perfect) Mold

*"One may no more live in the world without picking up the (moral) prejudices of the world than one will be able to go to hell without perspiring."*

*H.L. Mencken*

At any given time, men and women have been expected to conform to standards of universal beauty. The full-figured woman, living during the period when models like Twiggy were considered great beauties, was sadly out of luck. Similarly, a woman with a streamlined figure was considered undernourished in the Victorian world of the Gibson Girl.

To some extent, men too must deal with the same prejudices when it comes to body image. The short man, thin man, lanky man, heavy set man, and overly muscular man all feel the pressure to conform to today's ideal–the chiseled, tanned, and perfectly-proportioned model scowling at us from fashion shots in a clothing catalogue.

If your man is not an incarnation of a Greek god, you can make him aware of his best assets and choose clothing that will highlight those assets while minimizing any less-than-perfect aspects of his physique. In this chapter, we will examine the clothes that will be your best bet for a range of body types. Be encouraged; certain styles, cuts and colors can compensate for nature's oversights, and these strategies work.

# The String Bean – Tall and Weedy

*"A weed is no more than a flower in disguise."*

James Russell Lowell

Gary Cooper, star of the classic film *High Noon,* was the perfect example of a tall and lanky guy. Although we use the term "tall, dark, and handsome" to denote the ideal male image, a very tall man(if he is exceptionally tall and thin–may be perceived as awkward and gawky. Clothing can correct this perception.

## Best bets for the tall man (5' 10" and up):

- Jackets and trousers with cuffs.
- Sports jackets worn with contrasting trousers to counter his long vertical frame.
- Pin stripe or a chalk stripe suit patterns with the stripes set further apart.
- Suits of a heavier fabric such as flannel or tweed.
- Suits and jackets with larger patterns including glen plaids, houndstooth, or square windowpane patterns.
  *(See Chapters 8 and 9 for more on suit material and patterns.)*

## When shopping with your man, check that the cut of his jacket provides:

- Plenty of room through the chest.
- Gently sloping shoulders.
- Wider lapels to balance his lean frame.
- Flapped pockets set lower.
- An easy fitting waist.

It is also important that his jacket be a tad on the long side. When he stands with his arms at his side, the knuckles of his thumbs should bend at the precise bottom of his jacket.

## When your tall man tries on a pair of trousers, look for:

**a** Plenty of vertical room from the waistband to the bottom of the crotch.

**b** Pleats opening toward the zipper (forward-facing pleats), which his longer frame can carry, and which will provide him a comfortable fit.

**c** Fuller-cut trouser legs to accommodate his larger thighs.

**d** Standard trouser length with the bottom of the material resting on the back of his shoe at ½ inch above the top of the heel.

A tall man should also wear a more substantial welted shoe (the welt is the "side" of the shoe which holds the upper portion, the sole, and insole together). This conforms with his height and provides extra support if needed.

### Shirt selections should include:

**a** Solid colored dress shirts, including wide vertical stripes.
**b** White collars and cuffs to break up the extended length of his arms.
**c** Wider spread collar points to widen his longer face.

Generally, accessories for the taller man should make a bolder statement and can be a lot busier than for smaller men. Belts in contrasting colors will provide him with needed width, and pocket squares will add depth to his frame. Ties in strong colors with large patterns or wide diagonal stripes, as well as solid ties in rich textured wool or cashmere, will enhance his overall appearance; consider them part of his everyday wardrobe.

# In Short – May I Say

*"A little man often casts a long shadow."*

*Italian Proverb*

As I learned while a student at the School of American Ballet, a short man should never be underestimated. On Friday afternoons, a group of us would gather to watch the professional men's class. Edward Villella, a soloist with the New York City Ballet and the shortest male dancer in the class, made the most magnificent leaps of all. They were breathtaking. To our group of young dancers, he was truly a giant.

Even well-proportioned short men are generally preoccupied with not being tall. They can, however, appear taller by selecting the proper suits and accessories.

### Best bets for the short man (5'4" to 5'9" inches are):

- Suits. He should stay away from wearing sports jackets with trousers in a different color, which will only make him appear shorter. A single color suit jacket and trousers will maintain an unbroken line flowing from his shoulders to his feet, making him appear taller.
- Two-button (three-button if he is particularly thin) dark suits with thinly-spaced pinstripe or chalk stripe patterns.
- Fine worsted wool fabrics, or twill.
- Slightly padded shoulders, narrow lapels, and pockets with small, unobtrusive flap coverings.
- Peaked lapels with points facing up rather than down, bringing attention up to his face rather than down to his feet.
- Jackets with two side openings, or vents, rather than a single back vent to add vertical lines.

If your short companion is especially thin, maintain his vertical line while providing him with some manly breadth as well. Look for:

- Suits made in lighter colors.
- Suits with fuller cuts around the chest and shoulder areas.
- Suits constructed in bulky tweeds, herringbones, and flannels.
- Materials with smaller patterns, including horizontal windowpanes, or plaids
- A double-breasted jacket, as its double row of buttons will give him the illusion of greater chest width.

The correct length for a smaller man's jacket is of prime concern. It should be long enough to cover his derrière, but not be so long as to make his legs look shorter. The length of his sleeve should likewise balance the length of his jacket. Don't let a salesperson convince you that a jacket can "just be shortened." It will destroy the balance of the garment.

If he has a suit custom-made, ask the tailor to set the indentation for his waist higher in the jacket, along with its pockets. These adjustments will also give your man added height.

## The shorter man's trousers should:

- Fasten comfortably at the point of his natural waist, and not below.
- Feature pleats to add bulk, especially if he is extremely thin.
- Be held up by suspenders rather than a belt. Suspenders enhance the vertical line of his body. Only the short man who is very thin should venture to wear a belt, which should be narrow, in the same color as his trousers, with a small, inconspicuous buckle.
- Have a narrow and slightly tapered leg. If his trousers are excessively wide at the bottom, they will not only make his legs appear shorter, they will make his feet look smaller as well.
- Rest on the top of his shoes with a pronounced inward fall of the fabric in the front. The hem should gradually become 2 inches longer in the back of the leg than in the front.
- Trouser cuffs should be avoided, as they will cut the line extending from the trouser through the shoes to the floor.

## Tips for choosing shirts for a short man include:

- Dress shirts, in white, solid colors, or vertical stripes.
- Collars and cuffs in the same color and pattern as the shirt itself. White colors and cuffs on a dress shirt interrupt the line connecting the sleeve to his hand.
- Collars that complement the size and shape of his face as well as the size of his neck. For example, a cutaway collar with its wide-set points will look especially well on a man with a small-boned face. If his neck is smaller, his collar should also be smaller. If his neck is exceptionally long for his height, then his collar points should be longer as well.

Ties offer a great opportunity for the shorter man to create the critical vertical line. A shorter man's best tie selections should:

- Be in muted, low contrast colors, preferably striped or solid.
- Be no more than 3 ½ wide. Because a shorter man normally has narrower shoulders, his suit lapels should also be narrower. For this reason a narrow tie is appropriate.
- Never hang below the top of his belt buckle. There are tailors who specialize in altering ties. If at present he owns a group of ties which he loves, but must be tucked into his belt in order to keep them in place, a trip to one of these tailors would be a wise investment.

## Regarding outerwear:

**a** He will look taller in a single-breasted topcoat rather than a double-breasted style.

**b** Make sure that the coat is the proper length, from 2 to 3 inches below his knee. If a topcoat is too long on a short man, he will look as though his coat is swallowing him up.

If he enjoys sporting a pocket-handkerchief, the colors should be subtle so as not to eclipse his shorter frame.

Lastly, the shorter man should never let his overall look become fussy. His jewelry should be small. Subtlety and simplicity should be his motto.

# A Larger Challenge

*"Even overweight cats instinctively know the cardinal rule: when fat, arrange yourself in slim poses."*

John Weitz

Statistics confirm that the world population is becoming heavier. It is recognized as a sign of today's "fast food" societies. Still, throughout history, men like Prime Minister Winston Churchill of Great Britain–with a robust figure appropriate to the size of his expansive talents–have never let a little extra poundage get in the way. They always looked smashing, and so should your "well-rounded" man.

A good tailor and a well-cut suit are the keys to helping an overweight man look slimmer.

There are a few other things to keep in mind, such as:

- Darker, solid colors tend to reduce size (women know this fact accounts for the popularity of "the little black dress.")
- Smooth, woolen fabrics should be selected for his suits in order to minimize bulk.
- Narrow chalk stripes, pinstripes, herringbones and windowpanes will draw the eye up and down.
- Like the shorter man, he should create an uninterrupted line from his shoulders to his feet by choosing socks of the same color as his suit, or by wearing cuffless trousers.
- His jackets should move easily with his body, especially in the area of his chest, shoulders, and upper sleeve. He should be encouraged to choose garments in the correct size. Though it may soothe his ego to choose something in a smaller size, an item that is tight will accentuate those extra pounds, and also cause the garment to wear out faster due to added strain.
- The jacket should hang straight down from the shoulder with just the slightest hint of indentation at the waist.
- Pockets should be the more slimming flapless variety.
- Side vents should be selected over a single center vent on his jackets. Side vents will create a smoother line over his derrière and carry the eye upward from the vents on either side of his body.
- His jacket should be long enough to cover his derrière, but if he is also slightly on the short side, care should be taken that the jacket is not overly long. His jacket will also look better-proportioned if the button is positioned slightly higher.

## The trousers selected for a larger man should:

- Be worn at his natural waist ensuring that the rise of his trousers is ample enough for easy movement.
- Have either no pleats across the front, or pleats with openings facing the pockets. This will minimized any thickness through his middle.
- Be held up by suspenders rather than a belt, as suspenders will add no extra bulk to his middle. If he wants to wear a belt, it should be narrow, the same color as his suit, and have a small, inconspicuous buckle.
- Be cut fuller in order to balance his weight, and in order to follow the line of his jacket. His trousers should also be slightly tapered at the bottom.
- Be cuff-less as they help retain the unbroken vertical lines of his suit.
- Be offset by more substantial shoes to add support and balance his weight. If he has unusually large feet with enough height to carry cuffed trousers, choose cuffs to graduate the progression from his leg to his shoe, which will make his feet look smaller.

## The fuller face has special needs, also.

In shopping, pay attention to collars and ties. Specifically, remember that:

- A fuller face requires a larger dress shirt collar with longer points.
- His ties will need to be wider with a larger knot.
- Solids, muted colors, diagonal stripes, patterns and dots are best choices in tie patterns as they create needed movement that will offset the momentum of his body weight.
- Any accessories, including cuff links, watches and rings, should be unostentatious and tasteful.

He should also carry a minimum of things around in his suit pockets such as glasses, a wallet and keys which create bulk. If he has lots of things that must be carried, a handsome leather briefcase would be a better choice. Any briefcase he purchases should have a compartment for carrying such small items.

# The single/double-breasted jacket debate: Should he or shouldn't he?

There is some argument as to whether a heavy-set man should wear a double-breasted suit. Those in favor point out that a double-breasted jacket hides a larger middle, and that its double line of buttons draws the observer's eye away from his heavier central area. (A single-breasted jacket, if even a little too tight, will pull at the waist and only accentuate an oversized stomach.) Additionally, the V-shaped asymmetrical lines created by the jacket's lapels where they meet at the center create upward and outward slanting lines which have a slimming effect all their own.

The argument against the double-breasted jacket is that the extra layer of material across the stomach adds unnecessary bulk, as well as that double-breasted suits normally come with cuffed trousers, which make a man look shorter. In my opinion, if the fabric is smooth and lighter in weight, and the man is of sufficient height, neither of these negatives should prove to be a problem. So go ahead; if he likes the look of a double-breasted jacket, buy it.

## The Ironclad Man

Arnold Schwarzenegger, movie star, former Mr. Universe and at present Governor of California, who is known for being better put together without clothes than with them, showed television viewers and delegates at the 2004 Republican National Convention that he can wow 'em as well in carefully selected attire. Believe it or not, even Schwarzenegger has certain clothing challenges because of his exaggerated proportions.

### Suiting the overly muscular man requires:

- A suit with flapped pockets and wide lapels. A "sack suit" has a soft shoulder and a roomy waist, and evens out the discrepancy between his shoulders, chest, and small waist.
- Avoiding the double-breasted suit. It adds extra width across the chest, which he certainly doesn't need.
- A jacket a little on the long side, with two highly-placed buttons for better balance.
- Lightweight worsted fabrics, as well as striped or herringbone patterns to minimize his overly developed chest, shoulders, and arms.

### To select his trousers, consider the following:

- Full-cut trousers with a high rise worn at his natural waist.
- The trousers should also be tapered and cuffed. Cuffs will divert interest from his upper body to the overall length of his body.

Tips for purchasing the athletic man's dress shirt, tie and shoes:

- A longer collar with a tab that fastens the points to one another under his tie will make his fuller neck and face appear thinner.
- His dress shirt patterns should include bold stripes and vertical patterns.
- Tie selections are not limited. For the athletic man, they can be striped, patterned or even solid.
- He will require heavier looking shoes, in order to balance out his added mass and broad shoulders.

## Trust the Classics

Every year, fashion designers introduce men to a new variety of fashion flavors, but it is the traditional cuts and colors in men's suits, jackets, trousers, shirts and ties that continue to win over the hearts and wallets of the public. For this reason you need have no concern about finding the styles and colors that best suit your man's body type when you stick to the classics, a version of which is always available for men of all shapes and sizes.

# For Highlighting Assets and Minimizing Liabilities

## THE VERY TALL MAN

| General | Trousers | Shirts | Ties | Accessories |
|---|---|---|---|---|
| Sports jackets | Lots of room in the rise | Solids | Solid and bold colors | Shoes: *Substantial welted* |
| Contrasting trousers | Forward facing pleats | Wide vertical stripes | Larger patterns | |
| Heavy fabrics | Fuller cut legs | White collar and cuffs | | Belts: *Contrasting colors* |
| Large patterns | Standard length, ½ inch above heel of shoe | Spread collar with longer points | | Pocket square |
| Wide pin/chalk stripes | | | | Jewelry: *Large and prominent* |
| Minimal shoulder padding | Cuffs | | | |
| Longer jackets | | | | |
| Wider lapels | | | | |
| Lower set flapped pockets | | | | |

## THE VERY SHORT MAN

| General | Trousers | Shirts | Ties | Accessories |
|---|---|---|---|---|
| Single color two button suits | Fasten at natural waist | White solid colors or vertical stripes | Muted, low contrast striped or solid colors. | Shoes: *Lighter welted* |
| Smooth woolens | Pleats | Wide set smaller collar | Width never over 3½ inches | Suspenders *or narrow same color belt.* |
| Semi-padded shoulders | Narrow tapered legs | No white collar and cuffs | | Pocket square *in subtle colors and patterns* |
| Narrow peaked lapels | Longer length, 2 inches longer in back | | | Jewelry: *Small and simple* |
| High jacket indentation and flapped pockets | | | | Outerwear: *Single breasted coat, Length 2 to 3 inches below knees* |
| Side vents | | | | |
| Narrow pin/chalk stripes | | | | |
| Jacket just covers derriére | | | | |

# THE HEAVY-SET MAN

| General | Trousers | Shirts | Ties | Accessories |
|---|---|---|---|---|
| Dark, solid or narrow vertical striped suits with slight indentation at waist | Fastens at natural waist | Larger shirt collar with longer points | Larger and wider ties in solid, muted shades with diagonal stripes, patterns, or dots. | Shoes: *Substantial welt* If taller he can wear a trouser cuff to make his feet appear smaller |
| Smooth woolens | Pleats that open toward the pockets or no pleats | | | |
| Double or single breasted jackets | Legs cut fuller and slightly tapered | | | Suspenders: *preferred* |
| Flapless pockets | No cuffs | | | Cuff links, Watches, Rings: *Moderate size* |
| Side vents | | | | |
| Jacket length to cover derriére | | | | |

# THE OVERLY MUSCULAR MAN

| General | Trousers | Shirts | Ties | Accessories |
|---|---|---|---|---|
| Single breasted suits with soft shoulders and roomy waist | High cut rise | Solids and vertical patterns | No limit to his choices: Striped, patterned or solids | Shoes: *Heavier welt* |
| Light weight fabrics | Tapered legs | Longer collar with tab | | Cuff links, Watches, Rings: *Moderate size* |
| Wide lapels | Cuffs | | | |
| Flapped pockets | | | | |
| High placed buttons | | | | |
| Longer jacket length | | | | |

# His Individual Coloring Book

*"It is not quantity which counts but choice and organization"*

*Henri Matisse*

Keeping color within the lines is as important now as it was in kindergarten. Even then, I'll bet, your man consistently showed a preference for a specific color crayon. Every one of us favors a color palette unique to ourselves, a set of colors that simply appeal to us emotionally as well as flatter us physically. This chapter is about finding those colors–or families of colors–that work well for your man and sticking to them with all future purchases.

## A Woman's Sneaky Little Shopping Secret

Every woman has a little shopping secret that saves her endless amounts of time. When actually deciding what to try on in a store, she takes the garment off the rack, walks over to the nearest mirror and holds it under her chin. If it doesn't bring out the color of her eyes, her skin or her hair, back it goes to the rack.

## Beware of Your Color Prejudices

You, the woman in his life, must be careful not to project the colors that look good on you on to him. Your man has his own skin, hair and eye coloring to determine what hues look best on him. No matter how many things in life you may share, suitable colors for clothing may not be one of them!

## His Dinner Napkin Triangle

In choosing the right colors for your guy, pay particular attention to those that will rest like a tucked-in dinner napkin just beneath his face. The colors found in his shirt, tie, and the lapels of his jacket reflect upward and must be selected to set off his features to their best advantage.

## Clues to the Best Colors

Take careful note of the color and the highlights in his hair. Repeating these colors beneath his chin will create a total frame around his face, keeping it the center of attention. His skin tone should likewise be noted. No matter what his ethnicity, your man's skin will be either a warm tone or a cool one. A ruddy, olive, or warm brown complexion will be set off beautifully with a tie or shirt with reddish yellow –warm–undertones. Skin ranging from fair and pink to cocoa to deep cool brown will look better in a clear red with blue undertones.

## Learning About Contrast

Contrast and tone also play an important role in choosing the correct range of colors to be combined in an outfit. Examine your man's skin tone in relation to his eye and hair color. If there is a striking difference, if there is a crispness to the color boundaries, he is "high contrast." If the colors seem close in range, and the overall effect is more harmonious, then he is "low contrast."

For example, a Caucasian man with black hair, fair skin, and blue eyes has a high degree of contrast in his natural coloring. He will look his best in a high contrast color combination such as a navy suit, white shirt and red tie. On the other hand, a man with brown hair, medium olive skin, and brown eyes will look his best in a low contrast combination such as a camel hair jacket, beige shirt and rust tie. He will be overwhelmed by highly contrasting colors. Remaining within his one tonal family, he should choose color combinations that are subtle rather then extreme. Caucasian men with tans in summer can always go with more intense colors and contrast than they can normally during the winter.

For Latino and Asian men, contrast generally tends to be high because of their very dark hair and eyes.

African-American men can be of several ranges. The best way to ascertain the correct amount of contrast is to hold up a stark white garment next to his face. If he has very dark skin tones, the white will provide a high contrast and he will look best in all high-contrast colors; if his skin is lighter in tone he will look his best in middle-contrasts; and if his skin is very light he will look best in soft-contrasts.

Gray hair doesn't necessarily mean a man changes from high contrast to low, especially if hair turns very white and he still has considerable amount of it. Older gentlemen of any race with a shock of white or light gray hair that reads starkly against their skin tone may still need clear, strong colors and high contrast in their clothing. Generally, however, aging does soften the contrast between skin and hair, so choose accordingly.

## Those Great Big Beautiful Eyes

Eye color is very important as well, especially when the color of the iris is distinctive. In this case, the color of his eyes should be repeated if possible in the pattern of his tie, pocket-square, or in one of the stripes of his coordinated dress shirt. Brown eyes have undertones of other colors such as red or green. Find out what works best by holding various solid colors under his chin in strong light, and choose the one that brings out his eye color.

## Reading Colors

The way color reads depends on the strength of light it's in. When assessing a color for your man, do it near sunlight where there isn't too much glare. When shopping, you should feel free to go to the window with a garment in hand to look at it in natural light. Natural light is always the best judge of a color.

Following these rules-of-thumb may lead to answers different than you were expecting for your man, but your eye will tune in to the new choices soon, and you will see the advantage of accommodating his unique palette as you build his classic wardrobe.

# II

## Proper Planning

# 3

# Attacking His Closet

*"Simplicity is making the journey of this life with just baggage enough."*

Charles Dudley Warner

Now that you have classified your man's unique body type and have become familiar with his best colors and color contrasts, you are ready for your next major step: ascertaining exactly what is in his closet, what should be discarded immediately, and what should be replaced in the near future.

This task is going to require all your patience and tact. His opinion on what he loves and the direction he takes in his own clothing choices should be respected and worked with from here on in. "He had convinced himself that he only looked good in purple, so he wore the same two shirts over and over again," says Marsha, of her handsome contractor husband. "The only way I could get him to wear any others was to rotate his other shirts to the middle of his closet while hiding these two purple shirts way off to the side." If your man loves plaid, make more purchases in plaid when a pattern is right. On the other hand, if he gives you the keys to his closet, so to speak, you can begin your creative–but difficult–job of putting together a classic wardrobe for him.

In any event, you will probably need his participation at least a bit in making decisions, especially at the start. You may need to steal him away from televised football games one Sunday afternoon so that, under your watchful eye, he can sift through and try on every piece of clothing in his closet.

Probably both of you will discover that there are a number of things he has outgrown–emotionally and physically. For example, if he has become a person of some authority in the community, he will have no further use for a pair of cut-up high school jeans, or a faded T-shirt from summer camp. Similarly, you will need to assess every article against his current status. Is he entering the work force for the first time, or moving up within his present company, changing careers completely, or simply adjusting to a new set of social obligations? Every outfit will have to be re-evaluated as to whether it should be retained or discarded. Anything that he has repeatedly passed over for the last three years, either because the color or the style doesn't suit him, should be donated to a charity. Check out the various worthwhile charities in your local area.

Once the winnowing process has been completed, he will no longer have a closet so crammed with clothes that on any given day he has no idea of what he has or doesn't have to wear.

From what remains, you can then take pencil and paper and make a complete list of what he now needs. Jot down the things that should be purchased soon, knowing that you will be filling in later. You are now armed with the information you need to buy for him selectively, and wisely.

*"And what would happen to my illusion that I am a force for order in the home if I wasn't married to the only man north of the Tiber who is even untidier than I am."*

Katherine Whitehorn

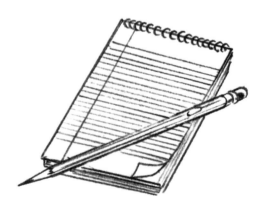

# 4

# Taking the Men's Department Plunge

*"Does fashion matter? Always–*
*though not quite as much after death."*

Joan Rivers

## Getting Your Feet Wet

Your first job as mastermind of his classic wardrobe is to get comfortable in men's shops or clothing departments–if they are new to you. One simple way is to venture forth when you are shopping for yourself. You are going to feel out of place at first, but don't let that stop you. You will find the environment highly civilized and quite refreshing, not at all like the craziness that we have come to expect in women's clothing departments.

*"All adventures, especially into new territory, are scary."*

Sally Ride

In the better men's shops, you will normally find salesmen, rather than saleswomen, waiting on male customers. This is not to say that female customers are not welcome. Quite the contrary. A woman who comes to look alone will most likely return, accompanied by a ready and willing customer.

Spend a few minutes at the most expensive men's shops as well as the less expensive. Ask yourself how the more expensive garments differ from the least expensive ones, both in richness of color, feel of materials, and in the way they fall on the store mannequins. Once you have observed attire from both ends of the spectrum, you will better be able to assess the right clothing shops for him based on his needs and his budget. Don't expect to educate yourself over a lunch hour. Give yourself several leisurely trips to learn to recognize quality, and to absorb the unexpected beauty of men's attire. You may be surprised by the pleasure it can bring.

> *" In the fields of observation,*
> *chance favors only the prepared mind."*
>
> *Louis Pasteur*

## Talking Heads

During this period, make it a point to observe what successful men are wearing when you spot them in restaurants, at parties, or on the street. You can learn a lot from television anchormen, who are always well dressed. Professional wardrobe consultants are extremely skillful at creating a positive professional image for their newspersons and talk show hosts. Nothing is left to chance. (Even when on occasion they make a really bad selection, you will begin to spot it.)

Ask yourself what it is that you find appealing about the way a certain man is dressed and if that look might be incorporated into the wardrobe of your special man on his budget. You are now almost ready to set a date for your first shopping excursion together, but first you will have to make an accurate list of all his measurements.

## My Guy's Sizes

The following chart for listing his sizes has been placed here for your convenience to copy and take with you when shopping.

# My Man's Sizes

Measurements you should have and take with you when shopping for him:

Suit/jacket size:
(His chest measurement)

Sleeve Length:                                    ❑ S     ❑ M     ❑ L

Waist measurement:

Pant length:
(His inseam measurement. The waist size will always be
listed before pant length on the size indicator.)

Dress shirt size:
(Combining his neck size and the length of his sleeve. The
sleeve length is located under the neck size and is shown as
a range of size, for example 32/33 inches.)

Casual wear shirts and pullovers:                ❑ S         ❑ M
(These normally come in standard sizes: small, medium,
large, or extra large.)                          ❑ L         ❑ XL

Shoe size:                                       Length
(Don't forget to include the width as well.)     Width

Socks size:
(The size of his socks is always in relation to his shoe size.
Refer to the size chart on the socks label if helpful.)

Tie length:
(Yes, ties do come in lengths–Tall (or long) and Regular (or    ❑ Tall
standard). This is not of concern unless you are buying a tie
for an extremely tall man or a professional basketball player.  ❑ Standard
Most men wear a regular length tie.)

Outerwear size:
(All outer coats should be gauged while wearing a suit.)

Glove size:

Belt size:
(His belt size will be one size larger that his trouser
waistband size.)

Other:

In order to ascertain these sizes you will need to do a bit of creative measuring.

## His chest measurement

Reaching under his arms, measure across his back at the level of his shoulder blades, bringing your tape measure forward to meet at the center of his breastbone.

## His sleeve measurement

His arms should be at his sides, relaxed but slightly bent. Begin measuring from the center point at the back of his neck, over his shoulder, down the outside of his arm to his wrist.

## His neck measurement

Find a favorite shirt that fits him comfortably. Lay the collar out on a table and measure the inside from the collar button on one side to the corresponding buttonhole on the other.

## His waist measurement

Making sure that he is not holding in his stomach unnaturally and with his hands resting comfortably at his sides, reach under his arms and measure loosely around his natural waist at a level just below his bellybutton.

## His inseam measurement

The distance from the top of his crotch to the top of his shoe is referred to as his "inseam." While he is standing straight, have him hold one end of the tape measure at the top of his crotch while you measure the distance along the inside of his leg to his shoe.

## His hand measurement

Lay his hand out flat and measure the distance around his hand at knuckle level from the outside edge of his index finger to the outside edge of his pinky, excluding his thumb. This distance in inches will be the size of his gloves.

## His foot measurement

Have him stand on a piece of paper while you trace a line around both of his feet. Measure the length between his longest toe and his heel as well as the widest point of each foot. Take the measurements in inches from his largest foot, which is normally the foot opposite his dominant hand, and use these two figures as your guide

*"Great discoveries and improvements invariably involve the cooperation of many minds."*

*Alexander Graham Bell*

## Why He Needs You

When men are still little boys they rely on their mothers to choose their clothing for them. This situation persists pretty much throughout their entire childhood well into their teenage years. When my husband left for Oberlin Music College, one of the last things his mother said to him before seeing him off on the train was: "Don't forget, dear, you look good in brown."

Without any real training to fall back on, it is not difficult to understand why men are forced to transfer this awesome responsibility for choosing clothing on to their wives, girl friends, or trusted female confidants.

## Going Solo

When you have the go-ahead, shopping for your man might work better than taking him with you–or he taking you.

Take Judy, for instance. She buys all the clothing for her husband Rick. He is a busy, high-powered executive who runs his own investment firm. "It's really quite simple," she says. "He knows a lot about successfully delegating authority, and he trusts my taste implicitly."

## His Time, This Time

If you decide to go shopping together, don't make the mistake of shopping for husbands or men friends and then dragging them around for hour upon hour buying clothes for yourself. All men want the women in their life to look attractive, but they prefer that she do the "putting it all together" on her own time.

When you do go shopping with him, make it totally his day, and be sensitive to his shopping style, which is different than a woman's. "The secret to shopping with my fiancé is organization," Mona tells me. "I decide first what he needs. Then I sit him down and tell him what we are buying, and where we are buying it, and how long it will take. Having set the parameters, he comes along willingly." Men are not always as into browsing and making up their minds as they go along as we women are.

*"I just put on what the lady says. I've been married three times, so I've had lots of supervision."*

*Upton Sinclair*

Every couple is unique, but if, like Mona, you can make shopping for him a really positive and time effective experience, you will be starting off on the right foot. He might even surprise you by treating you to lunch afterward!

## Anytime Is Not the Right Time for Shopping

It is always preferable to go shopping together earlier in the day. The salesperson is fresher, and so are you. It is also important to have waited several hours if he has had a large breakfast, especially if you are shopping for trousers. Doing your shopping in the early evening just before a shop is closing is an equally bad idea. Salespeople have families, too. You can't expect them to give you quality time and personal service while they are trying to complete the closing-time paper work.

## Never a Moody Man

Likewise, if your partner is feeling a little stressed or blue, suggest a trip to the gym together rather than shopping. If he is feeling low, he is more likely to make an impulse purchase. Likewise, if he is overly excited about a promotion or a recent business deal, temper his purchases as they could easily exceed his needs and his means!

.

# III

## The Consummate Menswear Consumer

5

# Salespersons

> *"A customer is the most important person in any business. A customer is not an interruption of our work, but the purpose of it."*
>
> *Anonymous*

## That Personal Touch

When I was a little girl, my mother shopped for all her clothing at a women's boutique called Johnson & Hare, which was very near our home. There was a special salesperson there named Tommie who knew my mother's taste and wardrobe so well that, in an emergency, she could literally select for her a scarf or shawl to her satisfaction and drop it off at our house on her way home from work. I remember, too, my annual holiday shopping trips to Johnson & Hare. While my mother was busy in another part of the shop, Tommie would secretly and painstakingly help me select just the right Christmas gift for my mother.

A good salesperson will not only look out for you in many personal ways, he or she can save you endless hassles and a lot of wasted time and money.

> *"Any activity becomes creative when the doer cares about doing it right, or doing it better."*
>
> *John Updike*

It saddens me to realize that today salespersons like Tommie are few and far between. We live in a world of super-sized shopping emporiums where you are as likely to get a salesperson just transferred from housewares, as you are to find someone skilled in selecting and correctly fitting an article of men's clothing. You will give yourself a better chance of success by patronizing a men's specialty shop, or the men's department of a larger, well-respected department store. These are the kinds of establishments that take pride in training salespersons in the art of selling specific merchandise. A men's clothing outlet can also have a trained staff, but there may be fewer on the sales floor for you to work with.

## Playing Your Part

When shopping for a particular article of clothing, both of you should be dressed as though you could easily afford to buy it. The minute you enter a men's department you may well be assessed by the sales staff. There is an instant decision as to whether or not you are worthy of their undivided attention. Salespersons are generally street smart. They sink or swim based on the size of their commissions. Any salesperson who decides to approach you should be treated with courtesy. You are never, however, locked into working with the first person who approaches you. It is your money and it is you who should do the selecting in all areas of the transaction.

## Your Power As a Woman

Salespersons in a men's department are well aware that when a woman is shopping with a man, 75 percent of the time it is the woman who will ultimately influence the decision to purchase or not to purchase an item. You as the woman engender unlimited attention and rightful authority. Use it. Actively help your salesperson to be of assistance. Show that you are knowledgeable about your intended purchases. If you are commanding and demanding, while retaining a pleasant manner, you will receive superior service.

## A Keeper

There are unmistakable signs that will help you distinguish the experienced salesperson from the inexperienced one. The experienced salesperson, after listening attentively to your request, will immediately go to the rack and pick out a garment that will fit perfectly without having to ask your man's size. If the shop doesn't happen to carry the garment he is seeking, a good salesperson will often suggest an alternative, but will never put down his first request.

Most often, a salesperson will start by showing the best of what you are both seeking and work down from there in cost and quality. Contrary to popular belief, a larger sales commission for the salesperson is not the primary motivation for this behavior, but rather it is a desire to make the customer look his very best. For this reason it is always a good idea right up front to let your salesperson know the price range that is being considered. With this information as a guide something more appropriate can be selected.

Don't be surprised if your salesperson asks your man about his profession or the kinds of social affairs he is most likely to attend. The answers to these questions are of great value to a seasoned salesperson and will help him to make additional helpful recommendations.

*"The important thing is not to stop questioning."*

*Albert Einstein*

## A Loser

If a salesperson addresses only your man while he ignores you, talks like a know-it-all, compliments ingenuously or insults excessively, and exhibits little patience for answering your questions, lose him promptly. Beware, as well, of a salesperson who tries to talk your man into a garment requiring excessive alterations, or one that can be purchased "on sale" only today. If it is obvious to you that your salesperson has put little effort into his own appearance, or is dressed in a manner inconsistent with good taste, continue looking until you spot someone who takes pride in his appearance and exhibits a style with which you can both identify.

As Oscar Hammerstein reminds us in his musical South Pacific (when it comes to a really good salesperson):

*"Once you have found him, never let him go."*

## Shopping Royalty

If, during your shopping expeditions, you discover a fine shop with a salesperson your man comes to trust and know on a first name basis, encourage him to become a regular customer of that salesperson. In this way he will be afforded all the advantages of "shopping royalty" which include the following:

**a** When a desired item from a favorite designer arrives, or an all-important sale is looming on the horizon, your man will be notified.

**b** In more exclusive shops, his likes and dislikes will be noted in a little leather book or in their computer, along with his sizes.

**c** Rush alterations will seldom, if ever, be a problem.

**d** If one branch doesn't have his size or color, it will be quickly found and sent over from another branch, and in some cases delivered to his place of business.

## The Value of a Good Salesperson

There is always more to be learned about quality, style, and fit from a salesperson who really knows his stuff. His assistance and initiative will undoubtedly shape your man's taste and enhance his confidence with each new buying experience, so take the time to cultivate relationships with the good salespersons you have been fortunate to find.

# 6

# Suit-ability

*"Like every good man, I strive for perfection, and, like every ordinary man, I have found that perfection is out of reach —but not the perfect suit."*

*Edward Tivnan*

## Suiting Himself

Purchasing a man's suit—more than any other article of his clothing—requires unusually careful consideration. The "suitability" of style and fit for your man will create a lasting impression with associates and acquaintances, one that he may have only one chance to make. And let's be honest, with a suit the most expensive item in his entire wardrobe, spending hard-earned money on a "mistake" is something you will want to avoid. Unfortunately, errors in judgment are more common than you may think.

Be smart. Ask yourself these questions before you shop with him for this all-important investment:

1 How formal or informal does the suit need to be? What do his employer, colleagues, or clients normally wear?

2 Does he fall into the category of the tall, short, heavy-set or slender man? Assess this before shopping so as not to waste your time or his patience trying on unflattering cuts and styles.

3 What colors will enhance his skin tones, the color of his hair, his eyes?

4 Is he a man who feels comfortable standing out in a crowd or would he prefer blending in?

**5** Lastly, what is the price range you and he had in mind for a suit? You will find it is better value to avoid the latest trends and stick to the time-honored classics.

The answers to these questions will focus your shopping and will help a salesperson to find the best suit for your man and your budget.

## Buying Quality

A quality-made man's suit is as much a work of art as anything you will ever see in a museum. Very much like an irreplaceable friend, you come to appreciate the beauty and value of a suit only by taking the time to know it in a more personal and intimate way. Therefore, let's get acquainted with important aspects of quality cuts and construction to help you buy the best suit you can afford.

### Choosing the Cut

There are four major suit silhouettes, each of which is suitable for a different type of man, depending on his build, his needs, and his taste.

# The British Silhouette

The first is the British cut, which traces its origin back some 200 years to a time when only royalty could afford to travel to Savile Row, a tiny street located in central London where, even today, tailors continue to create custom-made suits of distinguished style and quality. In the British cut, the shoulders of the jacket are well delineated, yet soft in appearance. The armholes for the sleeves will be cut high on the jacket for ease of movement, while the sleeves themselves will be subtly tapered to the wrist. The cut is also fuller through the chest, tapering to the waist, and then flaring slightly over the hip. High-cut side vents, which give a smooth line over the derrière, lend a dressier look to the British jacket. The jacket will also tend to be a bit longer.

British suit trousers are designed to be worn with suspenders. They have two front pleats on either side of the zipper and they are cut with plenty of room in the rise (the area between the waist and the crotch). You will find British-cut suits in both double-breasted styles with a double row of two buttons, or in single-breasted styles with a single line of two or three buttons. A British suit will also include a small change pocket.

Men, tall or short, thin or heavy set, should consider the British cut suit. It has lines complimentary to almost all figure types with the exception of the very muscular man.

## The Updated British/Ivy League

In the 1960s, Paul Stuart, another world renowned Madison Avenue men's shop, introduced a new and attractive suit silhouette, which combined the Ivy League suit with the flattering features of the traditional British design. This two-buttoned Updated British/Ivy League version includes a few vertical seams for more shaping, longer lapels, higher armholes, and a slight amount of padding in the shoulders. This suit with its two button closures traditionally fastens the top button only.

The trousers of this suit generally come with front pleats and, though they are still cut on the full side, they are slightly less so. This updated version of the Ivy League suit is traditionally manufactured in both a single and double-breasted version and is still proving to be an immensely popular silhouette at the present time largely because of its ability to provide needed room as well for the heavier set man and the overly muscular man, while still maintaining a graceful line for the man of average size and weight.

British Suit

Updated
British/Ivy League

## The Ivy League "Sack Suit"

The next suit silhouette is the Ivy League or "sack suit," a single-breasted, three-buttoned style which first came into fashion in the early 1900s. It was introduced in the United States to mass-market men's apparel by the world famous Madison Avenue men's shop of Brooks Brothers. Although this suit has three buttons for closure, it is accepted practice to button only one, the center button. This suit is sometimes referred to as shapeless (thus "sack") due to its jacket having no vertical seams to give a waist. In fact, the measurement around the chest and the waist in a sack suit can differ as little as 4 inches. The shoulders have a natural look and are for the most part unpadded, with loosely-fitted armholes. Its front pockets are designed with flaps. Instead of the double vent of its British brother, the Ivy League "sack suit" has only one single back vent.

*Ivy League (Sack) Suit*

The trousers for the Ivy League suit have no pleats. They hang full and straight with little tapering between the knees and the hem. This style of suit is considered to be highly conservative and very much the uniform of businessmen in the United States. It also disguises and compliments the figure of the man with a slightly heavier frame.

## The Continental Look

The impeccable Italians and French can be credited with the beautiful Continental (or European) silhouette. In the 1970s Georgio Armani became famous for creating this distinctive look in men's fashion. The shoulders are exaggerated, while the body of the jacket is single-breasted with softer lines and a snug fit. The suit jacket is shorter in length than either the British or American versions. The jacket also has higher armholes but no vents, while its buttons, as well as its lapel notches, are placed higher up on the chest. Another distinction is the design of its pockets, which are most often the sleek besom style.

Continental suits are generally made up in lighter materials and in more vibrant colors than suits made in the United States or Great Britain. The trousers rest lower on the waist and are cut to be more form-fitting. American tastes fluctuate wildly on the Continental look: some men find it a bit extreme while others find it very elegant. Personally, I like it.

Of course, the winds of world trade have carried various silhouettes to every corner of the globe. The differences have indeed become less pronounced, and you can find endless variations to each of these core designs. Men who are in professions that require a sophisticated, artistic appearance as well as men who are small, and/or slender in build, should consider the European cut.

*Continental (European) Suit*

## Size Does Count

Jackets purchased off the rack will be organized according to chest measurement, which is the circumference of a man's chest just below the armpits. The range of sizes usually runs from 36 to 50 inches. The suit trousers, which go with the jacket, will be shown on the tag as being 6 or 7 inches less then the chest measurement for the jacket. Men's sizes also take height into consideration, designating each suit as one of the following:

- Short, for men up to 5 feet 8 inches tall
- Medium, for men 5 feet 8 inches tall to 6 feet
- Long, for men 6 feet tall to 6 feet 4 inches
- Extra long, for men taller

You may find that your man will need a larger size if he is long-waisted or has a long reach.

# Single-Breasted/Double-Breasted

Wearing a single- or double-breasted suit is generally a matter of personal preference. Both are readily acceptable for most occasions, with only minor considerations to keep in mind.

For example, single-breasted suits are considered to be more casual then their double-breasted brothers. And, when it comes to sheer versatility, they can't be beat. The single-breasted suit is definitely the core model in most men's workaday wardrobes.

Unlike the single-breasted style, the double-breasted suit with its longer, peaked lapels, slightly tapered jacket, and more pronounced shoulder pads, is designed to be worn with all of the buttons fastened. It is, as noted before, the more formal of the two suit styles. Double-breasted suits can be purchased with two side vents or with no vents at all. Either way the double-breasted suit with its sharper lines is considered by the world of men's fashion to be extremely stylish and the height of good taste.

The man of average height and weight can carry off both styles. Even the heavyset man, as previously discussed, should feel comfortable wearing either. Only the overly muscular man should avoid the double-breasted jacket, as it will only give him added width across his already expansive chest.

*Single-Breasted*                      *Double-Breasted*

# Getting a Hold of His Lapels

The width of the lapel may often be the only thing that dates an otherwise perfectly good jacket or suit. The proportion of the jacket lapel to the width of the wearer's shoulders, as well as to his head size, is always a prime consideration no matter what lapel style is in fashion. Through the years, lapels have generally held in a range between 6 and 12 centimeters. A width of 3¼ inches is a pretty good measurement to aim for if your man's main concern is not having his jacket go out of style prematurely.

The lapel on a suit jacket can be made narrower by an experienced tailor. If the widest point of the lapel, known as the gorge line, is adjusted substantially, however, the collar of the jacket may need to be adjusted as well or entirely replaced, which can be tricky.

*Too Narrow*                    *Too Wide*

*3¼ inches*
*a good measurement*

*Correct Proportion*

# Pick a Pocket

The less the pockets stand away from the jacket, the dressier the jacket is perceived to be. Gravity, and the bulk of small objects in the pockets, is the quickest way to make a pocket sag and ruin the line of the jacket.

Jacket pockets should be used only when necessary, as, even in casual wear, they are often more for design than for function. If the pockets are lightly basted shut at the time of purchase, leave them as they are.

Let's go over some different types of pockets:

### The Besom Pocket

This pocket is built into the jacket itself. It has a narrow opening which is sewn along the edge. (When this stitching runs along both the top and the bottom of the pocket opening it is referred to as a "double besom.") If it is a "flapped besom," the man has the option of wearing the flap tucked in or left out. The elegant besom pocket is found on European cut suits as well as on men's tuxedo jackets.

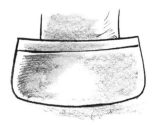

### The Flap Pocket

This most common type came into fashion in the early 1920s. The pocket itself is constructed inside the coat, with only a flap of material covering the opening. In a sporty suit you may come across an angled flap on such a pocket, referred to as a "hacking" pocket. It is often found on British-made suits and jackets.

### The Patch Pocket

This type of pocket with its highly visible seams is less formal than the flap pocket, often found on cashmere and camel hair sports jackets. The "patch" (a piece of fabric) is sewn directly to the outside of the jacket itself. A patch pocket will sometimes have a flap, sometimes it won't.

### The Bellows Pocket

This expandable pocket is constructed with three different pieces of fabric. Sometimes it is referred to as a "safari" pocket. It is meant to stand out from the jacket rather then lie flat. It is okay to carry a camera or snack in this pocket as it is intended for such use.

### The Cheat Pocket

Like an old-time western movie set, the "cheat" is all show with nothing to back it up. It is a false pocket, used as a smart design element while adding little or no bulk to the line.

### The Chest or Welt Pocket

This pocket is located on the left side of the jacket breast. It is slanted upwards toward the shoulder and is used as a receptacle for the pocket square. (A handkerchief subtly displayed can provide a touch of flair and color. More on pocket squares in Chapter 20.)

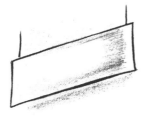

### A Ticket or Change Pocket

This, the smallest of pockets, sometimes referred to as the "cash pocket," is most often found on custom-made British suits. The ticket pocket is flapped and is located just above the hip pocket on the suit jacket. As its name implies, it is for holding coins, tokens, or theater tickets.

## Vents (Single & Double)

The single back vent in a suit or sports jacket has its origins in Great Britain as a means of allowing a jacket to fall gracefully while on horseback. Although its equestrian use no longer necessarily applies, the single back vent is the most popular vent in the United States and is most commonly associated with the Ivy League suit. When selecting jackets, bear in mind that the single vent may be economical for the manufacturer, but it is not the most attractive solution to the need for slack as your man moves about. When he reaches for something in his trouser pocket, the single vent exposes his normally covered derrière. For that reason it can detract from his overall appearance.

*"If the world were a logical place, men would ride side-saddle."*

*Rita Mae Brown*

Double vents are located on either side of a jacket. They are most commonly associated with the British cut and are considered dressier than a single vent. Double vents allow the man to reach into his trouser pockets easily. Moreover, they allow the material of the jacket to lie more smoothly over his derrière, as well as minimizing the wrinkling of the jacket in the back when he sits. Jackets with side vents are also more likely to hold their shape over time. The final advantage is that they move more gracefully over the man's trousers when he walks.

The double-breasted jacket will always have double vents or sometimes none at all. A double-breasted jacket will never have a single vent.

Generally, suits with a European cut have no vents. This ventless look compliments the man who is very trim. It is considered to be the dressiest and sexiest cut of all. The problem with a ventless jacket is that it tends to ride up in the back, becomes wrinkled when seated, and hinders graceful access to the trouser pockets. Thus, this style is not a good choice for everyday wear.

## Suit Buttons

The buttons on a suit are normally made of buffalo or reindeer horn, or mother-of-pearl. Double-breasted jackets have four or six button front closures. Single-breasted suits can have either two or three. Sack suits have three buttons, while the updated British/Ivy League has only two.

Jacket sleeves have four smaller buttons located at the cuff ¼ inch from the edge of the sleeve. Although four is customary, three or even two sleeve buttons is not uncommon. The number of buttons on a sleeve is the designer's prerogative as these buttons serve merely as style accents.

# Recognizing Quality

You can't be sure of buying quality if you can't recognize it. A designer label with a designer price tag doesn't guarantee a superior garment. Quality garments look better and last longer and, in the long run, provide better value than an inexpensive version of the same thing. Let's learn the signs of quality construction. (Throughout this book the important aspect of quality is re-visited in numerous chapters as related to individual articles of your man's attire.)

*"The buyer needs a hundred eyes, the seller not one."*

*George Herbert*

## Material

You can identify a good wool worsted by its soft, sensual feel and how it falls naturally and gracefully on the body. A good worsted will feel much like cashmere. Some very beautiful and durable cashmeres are actually a combination of cashmere mixed with other types of wool.

Feel the weight and texture of the fabric to determine seasonality as well as to assess its quality. Lightweight worsteds are a good buy as they can be worn for most of the year. Winter tweeds have a heavier, full-bodied feel, but retain their softness as well as their ability to breathe, thus are not restricted to winter wear. A foolproof test of quality wool is to crush it in your hand for a full 10 seconds and then release it. If it hasn't become wrinkled, you've got yourself a winner.

## Coloring

Dyes penetrate deeply into quality fabrics. For this reason, in expensive shops, you will find woolen garments in colors that radiate more subtle richness and depth.

## Matched Seam Patterns

The pattern on a suit or jacket (whether pinstripe, chalk-stripe, or plaid) should always line up perfectly at the seams, including around the pockets, where the collar meets the back, and where the shoulders and the sleeves join. Matching the pattern requires that more material be used when the suit is being made, resulting in a higher retail price.

## Interfacing

The interfacing of a formal "constructed" men's jacket is its main support or foundation. It is located between the lining and the outer shell. There is also a secondary interfacing area found at the shoulder of the jacket. Fashioned of woven hair (or canvas) and wool, it gives the jacket weight and definition, and prevents wrinkling.

Interfacing can be hand-sewn or glued into the jacket. Hand-sewn interfacing is the mark of superior quality in a garment.

Your salesperson may not be familiar with the different types of interfacing. Therefore, determine the quality for yourself by rolling the material between your fingers, observing how the slippery lining rubs along the outer jacket material. Interfacing attached with an adhesive feels rigid. Repeated dry-cleaning and excessive perspiration will cause fused interfacing to separate in time, resulting in bubbling on the outside of the jacket. You can minimize this bubbling on a less expensive jacket by requesting the dry cleaner to go easy on the steam when pressing.

Hand-sewn interfacing, by comparison, will flow easily between your fingers. The lining, the outer fabric shell and the interfacing will slide as three individual entities. An excellent confirmation of hand-sewn interfacing is hand-sewn stitches around the edge of the lapels.

## Lapels

Lapels on a quality jacket, aside from being hand sewn, should lie smoothly along the curve of the front of the jacket. A pre-shrunk tape of cotton twill, sewn inside the lapel, will add sharpness to the edges and help carry the jacket's lines. Wrinkles or puckers should not be present.

## Shoulder Pads

Shoulder pads are constructed of several layers of cotton padding encased in muslin (a sturdy, plain-weave cotton). They should flatter your man's build in a subtle way. Exaggerated shoulder pads will make a man's head look small and out of proportion to his physique.

## Sleeve Head

Durability is necessary at the point where the sleeve meets the shoulder. Therefore, in quality garments, a piece of cotton or lamb's wool, reinforced with canvas interfacing, is sewn into place. This piece of cotton also lends a more graceful fall to the sleeve. A quality fit means the sleeve tapers comfortably from the shoulder to the wrist. If it becomes too tight, it will "grab" at the elbow when the wearer bends his arm. Look for sleeves cut high in the jacket as they increase arm mobility.

## Under Collar Padding

On the underside of a quality jacket collar you will find two materials of the same or similar color as the jacket. French canvas (a form of linen) and melton (a very strong wool) are sewn together to give the collar increased weight and a clean, sharp line. French canvas is often used in the shoulder area of jackets as well for additional body.

## The Lining

Linings that are lightweight and resilient are normally made of silk or rayon. Bemberg rayon is one of the best materials in use. Its slippery quality helps the wearer get in and out of the jacket easily and quickly. A better quality jacket will have lining in the chest, sleeves and back. The lining at the back of the coat will have a turned-under hem sewn loosely ¼ inch above the jacket hem.

## Pockets

Make sure pockets are positioned in keeping with the proportions of the jacket. On good jackets all pockets lie smoothly against the front without wrinkling or bunching. In addition, the tops of both front pockets should line up directly with the jacket's center button.

## Buttons

The buttons on a good suit, as previously noted, will be made of buffalo or reindeer horn, or mother-of-pearl. (Leather, ceramic or brass buttons are most commonly found on sports jackets and blazers.) Ground natural horn is also combined with resin in some cases. The best buttons are also "domed" in the back. This shape helps the button slip more easily in and out of the buttonhole. In the best garments, the buttons are sewn on by hand in parallel stitches. Machine-sewn buttons are sewn with an X-pattern. Buttons should be sewn on securely, while maintaining some play between the fabric and the button for ease in buttoning. There is nothing worse than bringing a garment home only to find that a button falls off with the first wearing. Ask the in-house tailor to reinforce loose buttons if necessary.

Jacket sleeve buttons should be positioned just touching each other with working buttonholes, which are one-half of the diameter of the button plus an extra ⅛ inch. Spare buttons should also be provided on a quality garment. They will be found stitched to the inside of the suit or pinned to it in a little plastic bag.

## The Value of Hand-Stitching

Hand-stitching is the most obvious sign of quality workmanship and is extremely desirable. Hand-stitched jackets look better and will hold their shape longer. Note that, in certain parts of a jacket, the hand-stitching may be uneven, adjusting size for stress points where more flexibility and resistance are needed.

Hand-sewn buttons and buttonholes are likewise superior. The tiny stitches around a hand-sewn buttonhole can be a work of art. Hand-stitching is also found along the bottom seam of a jacket's lining and, as mentioned previously, along the outer edge of the lapels and underneath the collar.

In spite of the many technical achievements of the modern age, suits constructed by tailors in custom shops around the world still do three quarters of all their stitching by hand. This is a handover from the past that can be truly appreciated by any man–or woman.

# 7

# Suit Materials

*"Our clothes are too much a part of us for most of us ever to be entirely indifferent to their condition; it is as though the fabric were indeed a natural extension of the body, or even the soul."*

*Quentin Crisp*

A suit made of fine fabric lends authority and refinement to the wearer. Shoppers should expect to pay a premium for suits made of superior fabrics, since the cloth with which a man's suit is constructed accounts for at least two-thirds of the cost. As with styling, choose a fabric that is the highest quality he can afford and you will have one happy suit owner for many years to come.

This chapter relates some of the pros and cons of the different fabrics used in men's suits so you can make the best choice for your budget.

## Wool

To become knowledgeable about suit fabrics you will need to know especially about wool. Wool is the number one choice for business suits the world over because of its many important advantages. It has an ability to hold its shape in both cold and warm air, is able to absorb and release perspiration, while its fibers readily resist rain during a passing shower. In addition, should the sleeve swipe the flambé, it is very hard to set wool on fire. (At worst it will only smolder.) Wool fabrics range in weight from 7 ounces to 15 ounces per square yard. Because men are less concerned these days with extremes of weather—moving from temperature-controlled interiors to air-conditioned or heated cars, trains and buses—wools in year-round weights of 8½ to 12 ounces per square yard are the most popular.

## Woolens and Worsteds

Within the general category of wool there are two recognizable divisions, woolens and worsteds. These divisions are defined according to the way the fibers are prepared resulting in weaves of varying snugness. Woolens are the more loosely woven, are soft to the touch, and create a rough, nappy surface. Worsteds, sometimes referred to as "cool wool," are characteristically smoother to the touch, stronger, and more tightly woven. Tropical worsteds refer to newer lightweight summer woolens containing even finer threads. Worsteds are largely wrinkle resistant.

## How Wool Is Graded

It takes approximately 4 yards of wool fabric to construct a man's suit. This yardage is designated by a "Super" wool labeling system. A higher Super number indicates a narrower width fiber, hence a higher quality fabric. Along with width, longer fibers are also considered to be superior Super 150 wool is the finest merino wool fiber you can buy. Also, the higher the Super designation, the lighter and stronger the wool becomes, and the better its drape. When shopping for a suit, the store sales label will tell you the Super wool grade and if it has been blended with other materials.

## Wools Used in Men's Suits – A List

Included here are some commonly found woolens and worsteds used for the construction of men's suits and sports jackets.

### Merino

Merino is the highest quality of all wools. Its fibers are taken from a breed of sheep of the same name which were brought to Australia from Spain at the end of the 18th Century. The wool from the Merino sheep is very wavy and very thin. It is graded as Super wool, designating a very fine material.

### Tweed

Tweeds are heavy, rough, woolen fabrics, known for their depth of color and lively, spongy qualities. They have long been associated with winter wardrobes. Three of the most celebrated tweeds are the "Donegal," with flecks of color woven throughout the material; the "Shetland," most notably in plaids and stripes; and the heavier "Harris," with its rich warm colors and herringbone pattern. Tweeds of equal beauty are presently being produced at one third of the original weights. For this reason, tweeds can now be easily considered for the warm seasons.

## Cheviot

Cheviot tweed in either a plain or twill weave is characterized by its rugged, nappy, lustrous texture. It is most often woven from the wool of a sheep found in the Cheviot Hills bordering England and Scotland, but can be woven from cotton, and manmade fibers as well. Because of its heavy, coarse quality, it is used for making winter suits  sports jackets, and overcoats.

## Gabardine

Gabardine is a soft, tightly woven fabric with strength and body. It holds a trouser crease, is virtually water and soil resistant, and is most often found in solid colors, especially tan. It can be worn comfortably year round due to its lighter weight. However, gabardine does have a few disadvantages. It's expensive, and may not be worth the amount of wear that he will get out of it. It requires delicate care; a high heat when ironing gabardine will cause it to acquire a permanent shine.

## Crepe

This lightweight material has had its yarn twisted before being woven. This gives its surface a bumpy feel and a granular matte appearance. When it is produced out of a top grade, lightweight wool, it works well for casual warm weather suits. It also resists wrinkling. This is the "signature" fabric introduced in the 1980s by designer Giorgio Armani. If it is made up in an inferior grade of wool, however, it can feel rough.

## Flannel

The "man in the gray flannel suit" made famous by the classic film of the same name has come a long way since the 1950s. Although it is a popular symbol of male respectability, flannel has broadened considerably in the types of suits it is used to construct, and in its various fabric weights. Chalk stripe suits are most often made of flannel, but you will find flannel suits to fit many tastes and budgets. A flannel suit should always be purchased with two pairs of matching trousers, as the friction created when a man sits for long periods at his desk will cause the trousers to wear out before the jacket. Lighter weight flannels can be worn throughout much of the year, excluding the hot summer months, of course.

## Cashmere

This superb fabric is made from the undercoat of the Cashmere goat, which roams the mountains of Kashmir, Tibet, and Mongolia. It is soft, warm, drapes beautifully, and has a luxurious feel. Cashmere blazers with their soft luster and subtle colors are particularly handsome. This wool is extremely expensive because the supply is limited, while the demand for it is not. When more threads are used in the cashmere weave, the fabric becomes even stronger and more beautiful. Single-ply cashmere doesn't hold up as well as a weave constructed of two- or three-ply.

## Vicuna

There is a familiar tale in the theatre world about the new actor in town who buys himself a vicuna topcoat in order to make an impression on talent agents, but is left with no money to buy any clothing to wear underneath. Yes, vicuna is extremely expensive. It is a beautiful, soft, warm fabric made from the fleece of the South American vicuna (llama), which is found in the Andes Mountains. For a time in the 1970s it became illegal to kill the nearly extinct animal. New methods of shearing the vicuna without killing it have made a comeback highly likely, at least on the racks of the most exclusive men's shops.

## Sharkskin

A worsted fabric with a slight sheen, sharkskin is generally found in darker shades with additional highlights created by the interchange of dark and light threads. It exhibits a "twill weave" (raised ribs running on its diagonal plain), and is meant to imitate the skin pattern of a shark. Although it is commonly used for men's suits, it is also used for men's sports jackets and uniforms.

## Mohair

The long silky hairs of the Angora goat produce this soft and shiny material, which drapes exceedingly well. It is most often used for making summer suits and men's formal wear. When combined with worsteds, it becomes highly durable and wrinkle proof.

In addition to wool, some tailors use lighter weight fabrics for warmer weather or casual wear such as these:

## Corduroy

Corduroy is a ribbed cotton material that lends warmth and is available in a variety of colors. It is most often used in men's sports jackets and trousers. The width of the rib, described as a wide or narrow "wale," will help you to determine the degree of its formality: a narrower rib is dressier than a wider one. Corduroy is a nice step up from jeans for men's casual wear, and it wears well, too.

## Velvet

Velvet is a fabric with a short dense pile on one side and a plain surface on the other. On its show side it is very smooth to the touch and gives off a subtle sheen. It is most often made from silk, rayon, nylon or cotton and can be woven in a plain or twill weave. It is used primarily for constructing men's jackets. Depending on the grade of the velvet, it can go from a man's informal lunch date to an evening cocktail party, which accounts for its practicality as well as its popularity.

## Poplin

Poplin, a fabric with a very tight weave made up of large, rough warp threads, exhibits a prominent ribbing. Historically, it has been associated with priests' ceremonial garments, and particularly with the town of Avignon, France, which housed the papacy during the 1300s. Heavier textured poplin is utilized for jackets and trousers, while lightweight versions are used exclusively for summer apparel.

## Seersucker

A seersucker suit says summer parties by a pool. For that reason it is an extremely popular fabric at resorts. Seersucker is lightweight, and always looks crisp in weather where everything and everyone else is wilting. It has a crinkled texture created by releasing and tightening the fibers as the material is being woven. Most often it is found in the color combination of soft blue and white; but the blue can also be replaced by soft gray, green, yellow, and even pink.

## Linen

Linen is a product of the flax plant. Its use in clothing can be traced back to the Bible. There are two well-known categories of linen: "Irish," with very long fibers woven tightly into a soft lightweight fabric, and "Italian," with a less predictable weave. In spite of its religious roots, businessmen do not wear linen "religiously" to work during the summer months, although it is indeed a summer weight material. Wrinkling is its biggest problem.

## Denim

This all-American material is not American at all. It was originally made in France over 200 years ago in the town of Nimes and was only later imported into the United States. As the fabric used in making jeans, denim is probably the most popular material for men's casual wear. It is constructed of weft threads with no color at all and warp threads dyed indigo blue. Men often wear a sports jacket with a denim trouser for a casual look, but this combination is generally inappropriate for the corporate world.

## Synthetics

More and more suits and jackets are being manufactured from synthetics, which are man-made fibers. Some examples of these man-made fabrics include nylon, rayon, acetate and polyester. These fabrics have the advantage of being lighter in weight, resistant to perspiration stains, and impossible to wrinkle. However, because synthetics are less prone to "breathe" in the same way a natural fiber can, if your man is bothered by overheating in summer weather, you might consider a blend, described next.

## Synthetic Blends

In recent years, synthetic blends have become highly touted. For example, blending various wools with synthetics has resulted in wrinkle- and shrink-resistant woolens. For good reason, these blends have become extremely popular. The blending of a natural fiber with a synthetic is proving in many cases to combine the best of all worlds: good looks, nice feel, with all of the practical advantages as well.

*"I base most of my fashion taste on what doesn't itch."*

*Gilda Radner*

# 8

# Patterned Suit Fabrics

*"Life forms illogical patterns. It is haphazard and full of beauties, which I try to catch as they fly by; for who knows whether any of them will ever return?"*

*Margot Fonteyn*

Unlike women's fashions, where the use of color, pattern, and texture is virtually without limit, men's suits and jackets for the most part are found in a narrow range of colors and designs. Color choice is dominated by navy, charcoal, medium or light gray, black and to a lesser extent, brown. Likewise, men's suit patterns are understated, although they do offer an opportunity for the expression of personality. The more subtle the pattern, the more conservative the garment is considered to be; the darker the fabric, the more authoritative and business-appropriate.

This list should make you familiar with the right type of pattern for a variety of business or casual occasions.

## Pinstripe

The most popular–and most conservative–pattern in men's business wear is the pinstripe, characterized by a crisp, pinpoint stripe running along the warp (vertical threads of the suit). These stripes are normally set ⅙ of an inch apart. Although they can come in any color, they more commonly come in a soft white, blue or burgundy on a charcoal, light gray, navy, medium blue, or black background. In the world of banking and the stock market, the pinstripe is the only acceptable pattern for a black suit, a totally black suit being only too reminiscent of an undertaker.

## Chalk Stripe

Another favorite and highly accepted pattern for the businessman, although not quite as conservative as the pinstripe, is the chalk stripe. This slightly broader stripe, also running along the warp of the cloth, is set ⅛ of an inch apart. It gets its name from its resemblance to the chalk mark line used by a men's tailor. This stripe pattern is most often made up in heavier flannel cloth with a background of charcoal or light gray.

## Windowpane

Although extremely attractive, the windowpane pattern–a light rectangle on a contrasting background–is not very popular with the off-the-rack market. For that reason, you will not see it often in ready-to-wear men's shops. This is a pattern you are more likely to be offered in shops that deal in custom-made suits. Because this pattern is longer than it is wide, it has a slenderizing effect for the wearer just as do the pinstripe and chalk stripe patterns.

## Glen Plaid

First, about plaids in general: plaids are box patterns. They are the result of dark and light threads crisscrossing one another. In men's garments, the plaids generally come in subtle color combinations, or the simple, popular black and white combination of the glen plaid. (Unless your man has exceptionally beautiful knees and you are shopping for a suit with an attached kilt, you will probably not be in the market for one of the more identifiable Scottish tartan plaids to which the glen plaid belongs.)

A glen plaid, like the windowpane pattern, may prove to be more costly because the vertical and the horizontal lines of the plaids must match at the seams. This requires the use of more fabric in the making of the garment than would be used otherwise. Glen plaids are usually made from finest milled coarse woolen fabric, which has a very tight weave. It can work well in either a formal or a casual setting.

## Tweed

As discussed in the previous chapter, tweed refers to a sizable group of rough-grained woolens made up of yarns containing many and varied colors. The diagonal lines running along the fabric's surface places them in the "twill" category. Tweed is normally associated with hunting and fishing, and generally roughing it on a weekend away from the big city. "Harris" tweed is the more hardy, roll-around-in-the-dirt tweed, while "Shetland" tweed is lighter, finer and certainly a better grade for showing off.

Recapping from the previous chapter, here are some wools that gained their name from the pattern created by their distinctive weave and textures:

## Herringbone

Herringbone's threads create the illusion of an upside-down and right side up capital V. Many people see this pattern as the pattern created by the bones of a fish.

You will find both suits and sports jackets made up in the herringbone pattern. This weave also falls into the category of twill.

## Houndstooth
This pattern is bolder that herringbone, and is most often found in black and white. The braiding of four white threads with four black threads gives rise to this pattern resembling a dog's fang, hence its name.

## Sharkskin
This is another twill woolen fabric with a very smooth surface. It has a black and white "salt and pepper" look. Sharkskin is sometimes referred to as the "pick-and-pick" pattern.

Other woven patterns pictured here include the Bird's Eye, Nail Head, Barleycorn, and Crow's Feet.

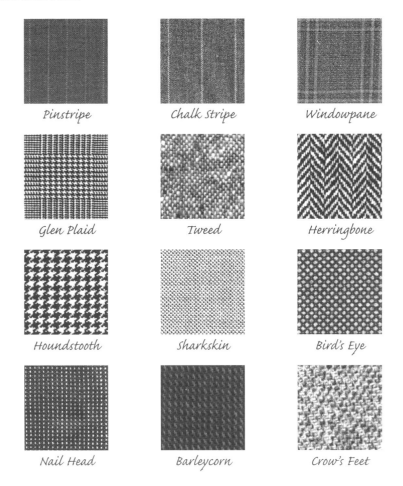

| Pinstripe | Chalk Stripe | Windowpane |
| Glen Plaid | Tweed | Herringbone |
| Houndstooth | Sharkskin | Bird's Eye |
| Nail Head | Barleycorn | Crow's Feet |

# 9

# True to His Trousers

*"You should never have your best trousers on when you turn out to fight for freedom and truth."*

*Henrik Ibsen*

The look and fit of trousers has everything to do with the suit they are married to, and their style depends completely on the jacket they are paired with. Specifically, they extend the jacket's cut–full or narrow–and are meant to sustain that look all the way to the floor.

Because of the integrity in a suit's design, wearing either the suit jacket or trousers as a separate never works.  Remember, that is rule number one; rule number two is to pay attention to their fit. The way they drape must not appear as an afterthought, and must serve to set off his smart tie and jacket.

Trousers should button or hook comfortably just below the bellybutton, which is the natural waist. If the waistband proves to be too snug–with little room for expansion–the trousers, no matter how nice, will hang in his closet and seldom be worn. Therefore, look for at least 1½ inches of seam readily available for "letting out" the waistband, across the back of the trouser, and through the legs. This is insurance for longer wear should he gain some weight at a later time.

# Two Pleat or Not to Pleat

Trouser pleats give a man extra room when he is sitting, thereby preserving the garment by helping to avoid undue stress on the fabric. Most suit trousers have two pleats on either side of the zippered fly-front, the inside pleat generally larger than the outside pleat. (The outside pleat is there to keep the inside pleat from opening up too far.) Pleats opening outwardly toward the pockets are referred to as "reverse" pleats. They are more slimming as they lie smoothly against the body. Pleats facing inwardly toward the fly-front are referred to as "forward" pleats, and are more commonly associated with British tailoring. Pleats created where the material comes together to form an interior pleat are called "inverted" pleats.

Trousers with pleats are considered to be dressier than trousers without. Likewise, if your man likes to carry a money clip or keys in the standard side or slanted pockets of his trousers, pleats help to conceal such items. Pleated trousers also have a more professional look.

Although trousers without pleats generally fall into the casual category, some European suits with narrower jackets will include them. It is important that these plain front trousers fit properly around the hips, as there is less room for him to comfortably maneuver. Corduroy, cotton, linen and flannel trousers often fall into this pleatless category.

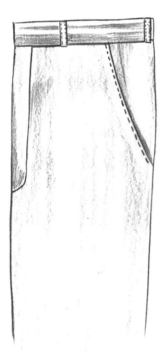

*Standard (side) Pocket*

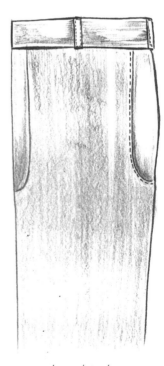

*Slanted Pocket*

*Reverse Double Pleat*

*Inverted Pleat*

*Flat Front*

*Forward Double Pleat*

## The Rise

The rise is the roominess between the crotch seam and waistband of the trouser. This area should drape well with plenty of slack. If the fabric is pulling even the slightest bit on either side of the fly flap, the trousers are then too tight.

The rise at the crotch is also designed to accommodate the side on which he carries his sexual organs. This preference is referred to as "left dress" or "right dress." Most men carry on the left side, and thus most trouser legs are constructed with a bit more width on the left leg. In a custom-made suit the modification can be made easily for either side.

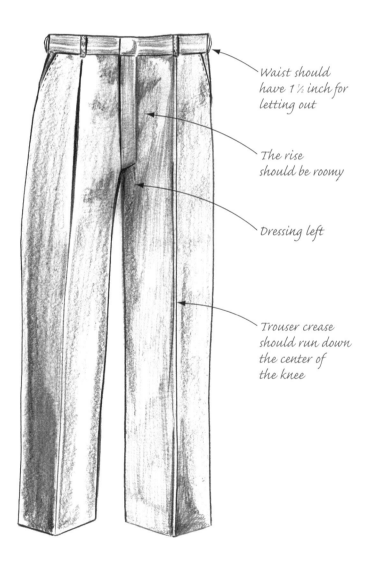

*Waist should have 1 ½ inch for letting out*

*The rise should be roomy*

*Dressing left*

*Trouser crease should run down the center of the knee*

## Tapering Legs

Trousers should hang straight and gracefully. Make sure that the contour tapers gradually from the waist to the ankle. The width of the trouser at the knee will normally run about 19 inches, while at the ankle it will most likely measure 17½. Note that the narrower the ankle, the larger the feet will appear.

The crease of the trouser fabric should be vertically-centered running directly over the knee. If it is off-center, the trousers are poorly made or in the wrong size.

## Trouser Length (Including Cuffs)

In order to have his trousers hemmed properly, be sure to bring along the shoes that he will be wearing with his new suit. Also, make sure he requests that a wide hem be retained after shortening. The extra weight at the bottom of the leg will improve the drape of the garment. The length of the legs should be slightly longer in the back than in the front, and the trousers should be long enough to cover ⅔ of his shoes.

Good taste dictates that there should be a break or "shiver", in the fabric toward his shin approximately 4 inches above the top of his shoe. If the trousers have cuffs, and most pleated trousers do, the break will be deeper than trousers without a cuff. If the break appears to be too deep, that is a sign that the trouser legs are too long. If the break is too shallow, he should ask that the trousers be made longer. Trouser cuffs usually measure 1¼ inches wide. If a man happens to be taller, the cuff should be made wider; likewise, if a man is shorter, the cuff should be made narrower. Cuffs not only help to hold a crease in a man's trousers, they also make the break in the trouser leg appear cleaner.

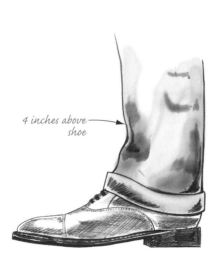

4 inches above shoe

*A deeper "break or shiver" with cuffs*          *A more shallow one without*

# Recognizing Quality

If you want to know the quality of a suit, look at the interior finish of its trousers. The more detail there is, the more expensive the suit. If the lining, which should extend to the knees, is made up in an inferior synthetic fabric, you can be sure that the entire suit will be lined in the same fabric, causing a man to perspire excessively. In order to keep the waistband from rolling, either hand-sewn or fused interfacing is also required. Look, too, for a silk or rayon lining on the knees. In larger sizes, lining in quality trousers will run one third of the way down the inside of the trouser leg–from the crotch to about the knees. This helps prevent chafing on the thighs when walking. Check for a strip of fabric called a "heel stay" placed at the back of the trouser legs at the hemline. This protects the fabric from wear and tear as it comes in contact with the back of his shoe.

Lastly, hand-stitching is an indication of quality construction in men's trousers, as well. Look for such stitching along the fly seam, inside the waistband, and at the belt loops.

## Trouser Fabrics

Trousers designed to be worn with a sports jacket or sweater are made up in all the familiar suit and jacket materials. Here are some pointers on what to look for when shopping, depending on what your man's needs are:

### Wool and Worsted Wool

With its smooth buttery feel, soft drape, and year-round wearability, wool tops the list of dressy trouser fabrics.

### Cashmere

Cashmere trousers are the height of elegance. Pure cashmere does not hold up well, therefore it is at its best when combined with another type of wool.

### Flannel

Flannels are first choice in cold wintry weather. This fabric has a nappy finish, and goes well with a warm woolen sweater or just as well with a navy blue wool blazer. It is most famous in gray.

## Tweed

Tweed is another fabric for brisk autumn weather. It is heavy, rough, and warm, and comes in solid colors as well as plaids and checks. For family winter holidays, encourage him to think tweed.

## Gabardine

Purchased in a neutral color, gabardine trousers are a good investment for occasions where something a little dressier than khaki trousers is required.

## Crepe

This fabric is sometimes ribbed, sometimes not, and is an excellent trouser fabric to take on a business trip. Wrinkles can easily be steamed out by hanging the trousers on a hook while showering in a steamy hotel bathroom.

## Cavalry Twill

This hardy fabric has both softness and richness. Cavalry twill normally comes in olive, tobacco, or beige, and combines well with a weekend tweed jacket.

## Linen

This fabric is used for summer trousers. It is usually constructed in a loose-fitting comfortable design, in a neutral color or off-white. Its only drawback is that it wrinkles easily.

## Cotton

Last but certainly not least, most men love, and live in their khakis (a strong cotton twill), their chinos (a lighter poplin or polished cotton), or their denim jeans. Each is a classic, and for presentable at-home wear, any one of them can't be beat–at any time of the year.

*"I have the simplest of tastes. I am always satisfied with the best."*

*Oscar Wilde*

# 10

# A Vested Interest

*"He who observes etiquette but objects to lying is like someone who dresses fashionably but wears no vest."*

Walter Benjamin

Most single-breasted suits come with a vest. This sleeveless short jacket, also known as a waistcoat, is generally worn under a suit or sports jacket. Since first introduced in England during the 19th century, vests have gone in and out of fashion, influenced largely by economic circumstances. During World War II, for example, vests almost disappeared because the material needed to construct them was directed toward the war effort.

## Close to the Vest

Vests have a classic, well-bred, old-world look. Aside from making the wearer appear aristocratic, they have a practical side: they provide extra warmth and they also keep a man's shirt from bunching underneath his jacket. In addition, because vests are almost always made of the same material as his suit, a man may discard his jacket and still look "put together."

As you are probably already aware, except in the case of "white tie and tails," a vest is always optional. Your man may choose to wear his suit without it for a more relaxed look, or with it as may be appropriate for the occasion.

## Construction

Vests have a buckle and a tab on the back to adjust the fit. (A tight vest is not only uncomfortable, but it will cause the tie and shirt to bulge out above the vest.) Make sure it can be made comfortable for your man. Also check that the vest is long enough to cover the waistband of his trousers. With side slits cut slightly curved in front, a vest should be longer in back, to insure continuous coverage of his waistband even when he leans over.

Unless worn in very cold climates, suit vests are normally made up in lightweight worsteds. Depending on the occasion, a vest can be constructed in any number of materials, patterns and colors. A vest's fabric is one place a man can show off the "fun part" of his personality.

*" Elegance is good taste plus a dash of daring."*

*Carmel Snow*

## Wearing the Vest

The only portion of the vest that should show when the outer jacket is buttoned is from the top of the vest to its first button. Traditionally, the bottom button of a vest is left undone. Normally, vests have two welted pockets, one above the other, on either side, slanted up toward the shoulder. The bottom pair of pockets may be flapped or un-flapped. Two of these pockets can be used for carrying a pocket watch and fob with a connecting chain falling loosely across the vest.

I am fortunate to have my grandfather's beautifully engraved pocket watch, which was given to him at retirement after 50 years of service as a managing executive with the Crowley's Milk Company. As a child, I remember him wearing it with great pride. If your man possesses a similar watch, encourage him to carry it and use it to check the time now and then. Aside from the emotional significance, it is a great conversation piece.

## Suspenders or a Belt

Suspenders are preferable with a vest as they cause the trousers to sit higher on his natural waist while eliminating the concern that a belt buckle will show below the vest. A belt will also add unwanted bulk to a man's waistline. By the way, suspenders and a belt are never worn together.

# 11

# A Man's Best Friend: His Tailor

*"Stripped of the cunning artifices of the tailor, and standing forth in the garb of Eden—what a sorry set of round-shouldered, spindle-shanked, crane-necked varlets would civilized men appear."*

Herman Melville

Nothing radiates success like a beautifully tailored suit. Simply said, the more powerful the man, the better his tailoring should be. By "tailoring" we mean the adjustment of the cut of the garment in every aspect so as to flatter your man's physique and bearing. Your eye, as you become more familiar with men's clothing, will grow more finely tuned to beautiful tailoring and you will, of course, want that for your man. For this reason it is necessary to know something about the world of tailoring as well as how to recognize not only a well-made suit but also a well-trained tailor.

## The Three Degrees of Tailoring

To begin with, there are three levels of tailoring associated with men's suits. The more a garment is made to fit a single individual, the more expensive the garment will necessarily be.

### Custom-Made

When a man wants perfection, he will spring for the exorbitant cost of buying a custom-made, or "bespoke," suit. For most men, this is a once-in-a-lifetime experience. Luckily, such suits, if well cared for, can last a lifetime and, believe it or not, have not infrequently been handed down from father to son.

A "bespoke" suit is created only after a lengthy interview with the prospective customer. At this meeting he will select the style, fabric, and color of his suit out of a vast number of choices. The cutter (the man who helps him with his selections and does the measuring), or the tailor himself (the man doing the actual work of constructing the suit), will want to know if he mostly sits in his job, if he travels extensively, and if he is required to attend a great number of social functions. It is then that accurate measurements of every part of his body will be taken. His measurements will be kept in a confidential file at the tailor's shop so that he will be able to order another suit without having to go through the entire process again.

A paper pattern will then be made especially for him. After the fabric is cut from the pattern, it will be partially sewn together, and the customer will be required for another fitting. At this meeting the garment will be adjusted in such a way as to accentuate the assets of his physique while minimizing any features that should be downplayed. There will then be a final fitting, until the suit is as perfect as it is meant to be.

## Beware

Just as in any really important decision in his life, make sure that your man purchases a custom-made suit only from an establishment with the best reputation. It is better to own a top-quality machine-made suit, than a poorly conceived, badly constructed custom-made garment.

## Made-to-Measure

In the world of "made-to-measure" suits, a man chooses the style he desires, as well as the fabric and its color. Likewise, he allows himself to be measured from head to toe before his particular suit order is written up and sent off to a factory where a standard pattern in his size is modified to fit his individual body type.

This suit will be expensive, but far less so than one completely custom-made. Many men, especially those who find it more difficult to find a good fit, will watch for a "made-to-measure" announcement at their favorite men's shop.

## Ready-to-Wear

A "ready-to-wear" suit or coat is the type of garment worn by most men. It is also referred to as an "off-the-rack" purchase. A suit will have been completely finished, except for its trouser length. An "in-house" tailor (employed by the store itself) will shorten the trousers to specifications and make any other minor alterations required. Although this suit may look very good indeed, it will never look as special as a custom-made, or made-to-measure suit, since extra room must be built into various parts of the suit to accommodate the largest number of customers.

My favorite success story in ready-to-wear suits comes from my friend Victoria. A non-profit fund-raiser, she helped her husband, Tommy, make the transition from elevator repairman to high-end real estate broker by shopping with him for several medium-priced conservative business suits and then having them altered at the best tailoring shop in town. "I would have challenged anyone in his office to tell the difference between his less expensive, but beautifully tailored suits, and those of his more experienced, higher- commissioned colleagues," she confided.

While a large part of the tailor's trade is making or altering suits, one can also have a tailor make adjustments to trousers, sports jackets, coats, even ties. There are establishments that specialize in custom-made shirts. The key is to find the tailor that you know does quality work.

## Finding That New Best Friend

The best way for your man to find a quality tailor is to ask a friend whose tailoring you admire. You may also limit his shopping to good stores with in-house tailors. These tailors have an intimate knowledge of their product, and thus are more equipped to do a good job. Your man will also have more confidence in the adjustments made before settling his account. You should also learn something about how a tailor works before having any extensive changes made on a garment.

### The Tailoring Process

Before a tailor begins to work, there are certain observations he is going to make about your man's posture and physique. Specifically, he will note the following:

a  Does he stand erect with shoulders held squarely, or slouch with shoulders rounded?

b  Does he carry one shoulder higher than the other?   (Aside from curvature of the spine, heavy briefcases and over-the-shoulder bags can lead to this condition.)

c  Is one hip higher than the other? Most men have one leg that is slightly shorter than the other. It is interesting to note that in 90 percent of the time a man will carry his right shoulder low and his left hip high. This condition is the complete reverse with women.

d  Does he have a flat or protruding belly? The tailor may take your man's natural, relaxed waist measurement before he has him step in front of a full-length mirror. This is not an accident–he knows that in front of a mirror a customer may stand unnaturally erect, and pull in his stomach.

e  Does his posterior lie flat against his body or extend outward?

f  Are his legs straight or bowed?

Should your tailor overlook, or your man fail to mention, any of these irregularities, it will be your responsibility tactfully to see that they will be taken into consideration.

A tailor's job will be made easier if you bring along the shoes, dress shirt, and cuff links your man will be wearing with his new suit. Don't forget to include things he would normally carry in his pockets: car keys, cell phone, money clip, or even a pocket watch. The weight and bulk of these items figure into small but important tailoring decisions.

A quality tailor will make adjustments in tiny increments of not more than ¼ inch. A tailor who is taking in or letting out a suit or trousers any more than two inches is suspect. If you have doubts about the tailor with whom you are working, ask a few questions to which you know the answers. For example, you might ask the difference between the cut of a British-made suit and an American Ivy League "sack" suit, or the proper length for men's suit trousers. If you don't like the answers, take your tailoring elsewhere.

If you do feel confident that the tailor knows his job, let him know your preferences, then sit back and let him work his magic.

*"Please do not have a fit in the fitting room. Your fashion life begins there."*

*Florence Eiseman*

## Common Alterations

In theory, any portion of a jacket or trousers can be altered. But in reality, only certain changes are recommended as they will enhance the fit while respecting the line and cut of the garment. Alterations, which can safely be done by an experienced tailor, include the following:

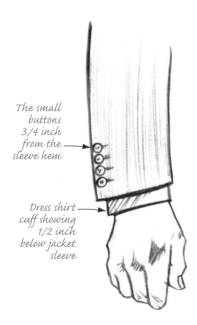

*The small buttons 3/4 inch from the sleeve hem*

*Dress shirt cuff showing 1/2 inch below jacket sleeve*

### 1 Adjusting jacket sleeve length

Jacket sleeves should hang straight from the shoulders ending where his wrist bends, exposing ½ inch of dress shirt cuff. (If he is extremely tall, make that ¼ inch.) The small sleeve buttons of the jacket must be no closer than ¾ inches from the sleeve hem. To accomplish this, the tailor may have to remove the last button, moving it to the other end of the row. Jacket sleeves can also be tapered at the wrist in order to retain the sleeve's correct proportion.

While my son Peter was growing up in New York City, he attended the Allen Stevenson School. A navy wool blazer was part of his required uniform. We mothers would start the fall term with newly purchased blazers. By the end of the year every boy had a crease mark at the end of both sleeves as we all, tried to make those jackets last an extra month or two before the start of summer vacation.

Fortunately, in better jackets, there is enough of a hem at the sleeves to lengthen them if needed.

## 2 Shortening or lengthening trousers

Shortening trousers is a standard operation for the competent tailor. Conversely, lengthening trousers, as with lengthening jacket sleeves, is difficult to do without leaving a horizontal crease revealing the original hem (as was previously mentioned). Also, to lengthen trousers, binding material must be inserted on the underside of the hem to give the trousers enough weight to hang properly.

*The break or "shiver" 4 inches from the trouser bottom*

To judge the best length for trousers, the leg should fall with a slight break, or "shiver," 4 inches from the hem. His socks and shoelaces should be covered when he is walking.

If cuffed, keep the width at 1⅜ inches for a man 5' 10" or less, and a width of 1¼ inches for a man between 5' 10"– 6 feet. Cuffs should be 1 ⅞ inches wide for a man 6 feet or taller.

## 3 Cuffs removed from trousers

There are a number of reasons why your man might want the cuffs removed from his newly purchased trousers, aside from personal taste. If he is short, removing the cuffs, as we have previously discussed in our first chapter, will make him appear taller by creating a continual line from his head to his feet. Bowlegged men also find this alteration especially complimentary. Once the cuffs have been removed, the hem of the cuffless trousers should fall with a downward slant, slightly shorter in front than in the back.

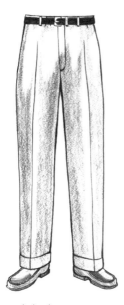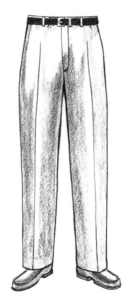

*Although both trousers are the same length, the trousers on the right, without cuffs, will make your man's legs appear to be longer*

## 4 Tapering or widening trouser legs

Most common in this category is widening trousers for the heavy-set man. For thicker thighs, as mentioned before, the tailor will attach a piece of lining that runs on the inside of the trouser leg from the crouch to ⅓ way down toward the knee. This is to ensure that the friction will not wear out the trouser fabric prematurely, or cause a skin rash. The silky lining also allows the inner thigh to glide easily, avoiding any bunching of the outer material. The natural center crease of each trouser leg should extend from the waist through the middle of his knee, and down to the center of his shoe.

## 5 Waist taken in or let out, with the closure re-positioned

If suspenders are to be worn with the suit, they should be worn during the waist alteration. The tailor will leave the waistband roomier to ensure that the trousers fall easily and comfortably around the hips. If a belt is to be worn with the trousers the tailor will want a belt worn during the alteration as well. A belt will move the waistband to a higher location on his torso providing a different waistband measurement.

## 6 Letting out the seat of the pants

If the fabric "pulls" horizontally on either side of the back seam, the trousers are too tight. Ease the tension by letting out the seam. Have your man sit in the trousers before approving this alteration.

## 7 A jacket taken in or let out

Good tailoring permits a jacket—closed at the center button—to follow a man's silhouette with varying degrees of indentation depending on the cut of the suit. No matter whether the suit has the more tapered look of the British or Continental silhouette or the fuller look of the American Ivy League "sack" suit, the jacket should still skim the body with just enough slack to give with natural movement. If the middle button of the jacket pulls, creating an X across the stomach, or if the single or double vents of the jacket "gape" when the jacket is buttoned, the jacket is too tight. Although it is acceptable for a man to unbutton his jacket when seating himself, a jacket should not be tapered to such an extent that he would be unable to sit with his jacket buttoned. Watch the tailor grab the center button of the jacket during the alteration pulling it from side to side. This assures him there is enough room inside the jacket for the body to move easily and gracefully.

## 8 The collar can be lowered or raised

A jacket collar should rest comfortably around his neck, allowing at least ½ inch of dress shirt collar to be exposed. If the collar is positioned too high, there will be a bunching of the jacket fabric at the crest of the back. It should lie flat. If the collar sits too low, the jacket will look like it is sliding down your man's back. A tailor can comfortably lower or raise a collar ¼ of an inch. Examine the collar itself to be sure it covers the felt backing underneath.

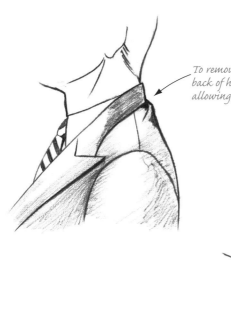

*To remove the bunching of jacket fabric at the back of his neck, the collar can safely be lowered allowing 1/2 inch of his shirt collar to be exposed.*

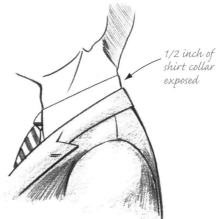

*1/2 inch of shirt collar exposed*

# Risky Alterations

Do not give the "go ahead" to the following alterations unless you are working with an extremely skillful tailor:

## 1 Modifying the lapel

We have already discussed the importance of the lapel to not only the integrity of the jacket's design, but to the way it should relate to the size of his head, the width of his shoulders, and his overall stature. Narrowing the lapel of a jacket is tricky. Take the word of only a highly experienced tailor before attempting such an extreme alteration and understand the ripple effect it may have on other parts of the jacket, especially the collar.

## 2 Making a jacket longer or shorter

Here again, there is the question of maintaining proportion. The length of a jacket, if well-fitting, covers your man's derrière, at the same time providing balance between his upper and lower body. Ideally, the hem of his jacket should fall one half the distance from the seam of his jacket collar down to the floor. Note that jackets are made slightly longer in the front than in the back to help the jacket hang properly. A skilled tailor will often consider shorting a jacket by ½ to 1 inch, but should not agree to do more.

Shortening or lengthening a jacket incorrectly can detract from its design, by making the pockets and buttons look ill-placed.

Lengthening is difficult because, besides crease marks, there is not enough material in the hem of the jacket to make it longer to any real degree. If a jacket appears to be too short or too long for your man, I recommend you start over with a different cut entirely.

## 3 Completely re-cutting a pair of trousers

This final and most risky alteration is an assignment only for a tailor with a great degree of skill since he or she will practically have to construct a complete pair of trousers from scratch. This is a custom-made alteration, and is seldom worth the effort or cost for an off-the-rack suit.

I can't say enough about the three dimensional art of quality tailoring. The partnership between a tailor and his customer is one of mutual respect and appreciation. Never shortchange yourself. See to it that your man is prepared to invest the time and the amount of fittings required to attain his own unique and flawless look.

# 12

# The Shirt on His Back

*"A genius is a man who can rewrap a new shirt and not have any pins left over."*

*Dino Levi*

To know what to look for in shirts, it is helpful to examine their function. Men wear shirts for warmth, and occasionally for protection from itchy or rough outer garments. For comfort, shirts must fit well and also allow air to flow to and away from the skin.

All these needs have been considered by shirt designers, but none as much as the styling. The look of a dress shirt is usually carried by the collar, cuffs, and numerous other details. Here is a glossary of terms should you need a refresher or an introduction to shirt fashion and construction.

## Major Parts of a Man's Dress Shirt

### The Collar
Perhaps the most important part of a man's dress shirt. The collar's upper layer is meant to show on the outside; its under-layer (or interfacing) gives it body. On a dress shirt, the collar is most often starched, and provides a perfect upside-down, V-shaped frame formed by the top rim where it widens away from his head while his tie, vertically placed like an arrow, is likewise secured by his collar. Both design elements give prominence to his most expressive body part, his face.

### The Yoke
The swath of material that lies on top of the shoulders and is sewn horizontally across the upper front and again across the upper back. At the back, the yoke can

be constructed of one solid piece of material or two stitched together with a central, vertical seam. This is referred to as a "split-yoke," which is preferred since it creates more room through the back of the shirt and is therefore more comfortable.

### Barrel Cuffs
Strips of fabric which finish the end of each sleeve. They can be constructed of double or single strips. Cuffs are closed at the wrist most typically with buttons, or in the case of French cuffs, held together with cuff links.

### The Sleeve Placket
A double strip of fabric sewn onto the slit above the cuff. It provides room for a man's hand to slip easily through the sleeve.

### Gauntlet Buttons
Small buttons found on the sleeve placket, which provide a means of closing the opening during wear.

### Front Placket
The double strip of material sewn down the center of the shirt, where the buttons and the buttonholes are located. The placket found in traditional, covered, and double turnback styles provides structural support for the shirt.

Collar

Breast Pocket

Gauntlet Buttons

Front Buttons

Gusset

Front Placket

## Front Buttons

Front buttons are commonly made from mother-of-pearl, horn or plastic. More formal tuxedo shirts fasten with studs, small decorative ornaments mounted on short posts that slip through holes in two layers of fabric.

## The Gusset

The triangular piece of fabric joining the back and front shirt panels on either side of a shirt near its hem. Gussets are found on a high-quality shirt, and enhance durability since they strengthen the garment.

## The Tails

The part of the shirt tucked into the trousers. It is important for the tails to be long enough so that his shirt will remain neatly tucked into his trousers even when leaning over.

## Breast Pocket

The pocket found on the left-hand side of a dress shirt. This pocket is strictly ornamental and should not be used.

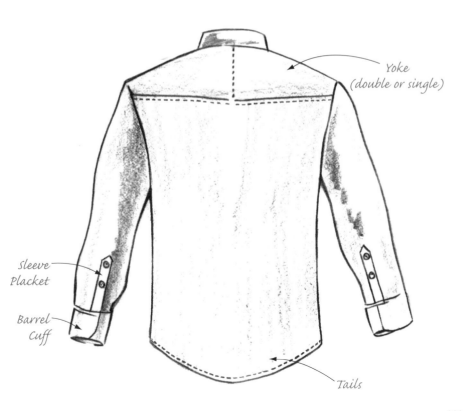

Yoke
(double or single)

Sleeve
Placket

Barrel
Cuff

Tails

# A Note on the Most Common Shirt Fabrics

Better men's shirts are constructed from the highest-quality, 100 percent Sea Island or Egyptian cotton broadcloths. These fabrics are tightly woven from long, slender threads, have a soft, subtle shine, and are smooth to the touch.

The name cotton originates from the Arabic word "qutn." Although the Moors, Crusaders, and traders of the East India Company spread this material to the far corners of the Earth, it was not until the invention in the late 1700s of the cotton gin, which allowed the seeds to be separated easily from the tufts, that the mass production of cotton became economically feasible.

Quality broadcloths, although easily wrinkled and difficult to iron, are extremely expensive. The less expensive Pima cotton (often labeled as Supima,) is also a fine grade of broadcloth from which quality dress shirts are made. Both these grades of cotton are comfortable, allow the skin to "breathe" and are highly absorbent.

Silk shirts also have natural and breathable fibers, but unfortunately, they have a tendency to hold stains.

Strong oxford cotton with fewer threads in its weave has a coarse-grained texture, and is highly absorbent. It is more commonly associated with casual wear. The finest grade of royal oxford cloth, however, can easily be worn to most social functions.

Let's now consider some of the variations of the dress shirt, and which styles will be best for your man.

# The All-Important Collar

The shirt collar–no matter what style you choose–affects a man's presentation more than any other shirt feature because of its proximity to the face. The size and shape of the shirt collar appears just below a man's chin thus enhancing or detracting from the most expressive part of his body.

If your man's features are delicate, and his head is small, choose a shirt with a small collar so as not to overwhelm his face. A large collar will make his head appear even smaller. If his head and facial features are large, choose a larger collar. If he has a short neck, choose a collar that sits lower on his neck. If his neck is overly long, choose a collar which sits higher.

# Six Basic Styles of Collars

### 1 The Straight Point Collar

The most popular collar of all, this style offers clean lines plus versatility. It goes equally well with 9-to-5 business suits as it does with weekend sports jackets. The points of this collar are 2¾ inches to 3⅜ inches long. This collar works well for the man with a fuller face since points being set closer together create the illusion of length.

### 2 The Spread Collar

Sometimes referred to as the "cutaway collar," this style was initially made famous by the Duke of Windsor. It flatters smaller-boned men and will also make a longer face appear shorter and wider. Since it can be found in many heights, with points of different lengths, and even with different degrees of openness, it is a perfect addition to every man's wardrobe. The spread collar, likewise, has the advantage of its points resting comfortably on a man's chest while being held neatly under the lapels of his jacket. This collar also accommodates the larger "Windsor" knot.

(Different tie knots will be discussed in the next chapter.)

### 3 The Tab Collar

This is a collar seldom seen in men's shops, but provides a very dapper air to the wearer. The "tab" refers to a narrow piece of fabric that connects one point of the collar to the other by means of a button or snap. This collar, accompanied by a tie, rides higher on a man's neck, closing the distance between his face and chest, making it especially worth seeking out for the man with a long neck.

### 4 The Button-Down Collar

This is America's contribution to the world of men's collars. It is distinguished by the subtle wave created when the points attach to the shirt with tiny white buttons. The button-down has produced an easy, relaxed effect in an ensemble, (since the early 1920s) and is especially popular for summer wear because of its softer and more comfortable look. Designer Ralph Lauren as well as Brooks Brothers are names associated with the contemporary oxford button-down shirt collar. Many a schoolboy, along with my own son, Peter, have worn their Brooks Brothers button-down oxford shirt and collar with a navy blazer to every family occasion. It is a polished, versatile look for boys from kindergarten through college.

So as to eliminate any confusion when requesting a button-down collar, remember that a dress shirt with buttons, as opposed to a pullover, may be referred to as a button-down dress shirt. For that reason, make it clear to your salesperson that you are referring to the collar of the same name.

### 5 The Pinned Collar

This collar lends a more formal appearance. In this style, the two collar points are held together with a gold safety pin or spring-like device (similar in function to the tab). It requires some initial practice to set the pin straight and centered. For that reason, this collar, though extremely popular in the 1930s, has pretty much faded from the fashion scene in our (always in a hurry) society. Because of its vertical lines right below the chin, and because it tends to ride high on a man's neck like the tab collar, a pinned collar is especially suited to a man with a long neck. It also flatters a chiseled jaw line or a full face.

### 6 The Rounded Collar

I can almost guarantee you will never see this style in any men's retail shops. It was most famous in the 1930s as the collar associated with Great Britain's prestigious Eton School. Those who wore it were members of an elite club, hence its nickname the "club" collar. Today, only men who have their shirts custom-made would have the opportunity to choose it. No great loss–to most men, this collar has a slightly dated look.

(The specialized "wing collar" worn only for formal dress will be included in Chapter 23–Puttin' On The Ritz.)

## Cuffs

Dress shirt sleeves have cuffs. Single or double-buttoned, the barrel cuff is the most popular, the double-buttoned cuff being the dressier of the two. The dressiest cuff worn with a standard suit is the French cuff. It is twice the length of a standard cuff and is worn flipped back on itself and fastened together with cuff links. A shirt with heavily starched, single-length French cuffs is the appropriate choice for a tuxedo.

The barrel cuff should fit comfortably around your man's wrist. If your man can get his hand through the cuff without undoing the button, then the cuff is too wide. To test if the sleeve is the correct length, make sure he can move his arm in any direction without the cuff pulling up the arm and exposing the skin at his wrist.

# Cuffs

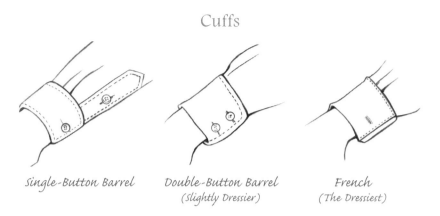

Single-Button Barrel

Double-Button Barrel
(Slightly Dressier)

French
(The Dressiest)

## The Short-Sleeved Business Shirt No-No

Whether winter or summer in a business environment, a short-sleeved dress shirt under a suit is never acceptable. A strip of cuff ½ inch must always be visible beyond his jacket sleeve. Where there is no long-sleeved shirt, there is no ½ inch of cuff.

## Determining Correct Size: Rule of Thumb

Shirts are marked in the back of the collar with the size of the neck preceding the length of the sleeve. For example; 15½–33/34 (15½ inch neck with a 33 to 34 inch sleeve length.)

For the shirt collar, the proper size will be two fingers larger than the circumference of his neck just below the Adam's apple when the fingers are placed inside and perpendicular to the buttoned collar. Note that even expensive designer dress shirts are known to shrink after multiple washings. Knowing this, some designers include this calculation when assigning sizes to their shirts. It is important, therefore, to ask your salesperson whether the shirt in question has been adjusted for normal shrinkage if it doesn't state so on the label.

The shaping of the shirt is important. Although it must be roomy enough to be comfortable, a shirt must not be so full that it bunches up under a jacket. Do not select one cut so slim that it pulls between the buttons. His correct sleeve length, if not already known, should be measured by your salesperson from the nape of his neck over his shoulder and down his arm to the wrist.

Just because a shirt is packaged, it does not mean you cannot remove it to try it on. If it is not the correct size, the salesperson can worry about putting it back into the wrapping. Do not be intimidated. Re-packaging shirts is a salesperson's responsibility.

# Recognizing Quality

To know if a higher price is justified for a dress shirt, apply the critical eye of a professional tailor. Be sure to look for:

## Hand-stitching versus fusing

There are two methods of constructing collars, cuffs, and plackets: hand-sewing and fusing. We became familiar with "fusing" in our discussion of jacket tailoring. Hand-sewn stitches on a shirt's collar, cuffs, and placket prohibit bubbling, at the same time giving the area a softer, more flexible feel. Over time, especially if done sloppily, fusing permits separation between the layers due to uneven shrinkage. Fused areas also hold in oil and perspiration, creating stains that are almost impossible to remove.

Hand-stitching found along the edge of the collar should be approximately ¼ inch from the edge. All stitching should be nearly invisible, and slightly uneven. Uneven stitches provide more give and take, extending the life of the dress shirt.

## Single-needle and double-needle stitching

The side seams on a dress shirt can be narrow and sewn with single-needle stitching, or wider with double-needle stitching. A shirt that has been sewn with a single-seam requires more effort, since the garment must be turned over and sewn again along the same line as the first seam. Thus, look for single-seam since it also minimizes puckering after multiple washings.

## Other signs of superior dress shirt workmanship include:

a  Collar and cuff tips matching in shape and length.

b  A yoke with a vertical seam down the middle in back.

c  Buttons of mother-of-pearl or bone.

d  Finished horizontal buttonholes on the placket of the sleeve.

e  Striped patterns coming together perfectly where the sleeve meets the yoke at the top of the shoulder.

f  Frequent, fuller pleats where the sleeve meets the cuff.

g  Removable stays in the collar to maintain crispness.

Expensive men's dress shirts are generally expensive for a reason. Still, don't let yourself be fooled by an inferior garment with a designer label. On several occasions, my husband, Jack, has purchased an expensive designer shirt, only to lose one button every time he wears it. Losing buttons (consistently) on a new shirt is a blatant sign of poor workmanship.

# Front Placket Options

 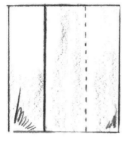 

Traditional          Covered          Double Turnback

## Some Dress Shirt Designers With Quality Reputations

For your convenience, included here are some names to look for when shopping for the well-made shirt:

- Asser, Charvet, Brioni, Borelli, Turnbull, Zegna (higher-end).

- Tom James, Armani, Burberry of London, Valentino, Lorenzini, Canoli (slightly lower-priced).

- Geoffrey Beene, Van Husen, Izod (well-priced, but still a high-quality product).

- Barney's, Saks Fifth Avenue, Nordstrom's, Bergdorf Goodman, J. McLaughlin, Paul Stuart, Brooks Brothers, Ralph Lauren (a few in the array of stores which carry their own quality line. These brands measure up well against the higher-priced designer brands).

## When a Custom-Made Shirt Is in Order

For men who have unusual proportions, a custom-made shirt may be the only answer. Custom-made shirts are normally twice the cost of ready-made and require a minimum order of four to six shirts. Economically it is not feasible for them to make one single shirt due to the substantial amount of work required. However, a custom-made shop, if requested, will take an order for a single shirt, but with a hefty surcharge.

Everything about a custom-made shirt is precise—from the selection of the color, fabric, collar, and cuff, to the measurements taken. The hand-stitching in a custom-made shirt is also exact. Since the buttons on a custom-made shirt are not readily available at most neighborhood tailors/dry-cleaners, the custom-made shirt customer will also be provided replacement buttons free of charge. Afterward, the shop will keep an up-to-date record of each client's measurements and preferences so that he can order a new batch of shirts by telephone or E-mail at any time.

## Monogrammed Shirts

For some men, and perhaps for your man as well, a monogrammed shirt is the height of luxury. Keep in mind that large monograms are considered garish. Should he wish to have his shirts monogrammed, see to it that the letters are no more than ¼ inch tall. Generally, monograms are placed on a shirt 4 inches left of the center button line or placket, or in the middle of a pocket, or in the middle of the pocket hem. The lettering will look best in a thread color that contrasts subtly with the color of the shirt itself.

## The Number of Shirts He Should Own

If carefully selected, ten dress shirts are sufficient: three solid whites, two solid blues, three stripes, a Tattersall (a pattern with a light background, displaying vertical and horizontal, two-colored lines) and an understated plaid. If your man is busy, and most men are, no more than one visit to the laundry per week is desirable. Having ten shirts will guarantee that he has enough clean options on any given day. If he happens to work in a casual environment, this mix of dress shirts can be modified to include more Tattersalls and plaids in place of the more formal solids. He should, however, maintain at least four dress shirts, preferably two of them in white, for away-from-the-office requirements.

*" Understatement is the path to distinction."*

*Oscar Lenius*

# 13

# Tie-ing One On

*"As rich in meaning and as expressive as a poem, a tie gives a man his own language."*

*Gary Cooper*

For over 2000 years, ties–of one form or another–have been part of male attire. It was not until the latter part of the 1800s, however, that the cravat, a scarf tied loosely around the neck with a large bow, gave way to the long tie we recognize today. The modern necktie, the "four-in-hand" (so called due to its similarity to the gathered reins of a carriage with four-horses) still remains an indication of the wearer's wealth, rank and position. Presently, more than 800 million ties are purchased each year by men, or for men, throughout the planet.

# The Main Components of a Tie

A tie has three main parts:

1 **The Apron**, or "front blade," the widest portion, which is displayed prominently down the front.

2 **The Tail**, or "back blade," the narrow piece which rests directly behind the apron.

3 **The Gusset**, or "neck band," the even narrower portion of the tie that goes under the collar.

The material used to make these parts is cut on an angle across the grain. This 45 percent bias keeps the tie from twisting when worn or hung in a closet.

# Tie Construction

When you turn a tie over, you learn something about how it is made and what to look for in a good tie. Looking into the back of the apron will reveal the following components:

- **The shell**, the outer "envelope" of the tie, which is made of silk, cotton or wool.

- **The interlining**, running the entire length of the tie, keeps the tie from becoming wrinkled, ensures that it falls properly, and provides the required body for easier tying.

- **The tipping**, a layer of fabric covering the interlining at the back of the apron on an expensive tie, may match the shell (as in French tipping) or have a contrasting pattern or color.

- **The main seam stitch**, preferably a hand-sewn seam, which runs down the back of the tie holding all the parts together.

- **The two bar tacks**, strong and tightly twisted bands of thread sewn across the main seam stitching just before the opening of the apron and tail, provide reinforcement at both ends of the tie.

- **The slipstitch**, a black thread approximately 5 inches long loosely basted with a knot or loop located at the shell end (or at both ends) of the main seam stitch, this essential part of the tie allows for natural stretching, relieves stress on the main seam, enables the tie to drape gracefully, and helps maintain its shape. The slipstitch isn't always visible from the outside, as it is often concealed in the lining for protection.

- **The fabric loop**, sewn across the back of the apron, used for guiding the tail of the tie against the apron and for holding it neatly in place when worn, is where designers place their printed or woven labels.

# Parts of His Tie

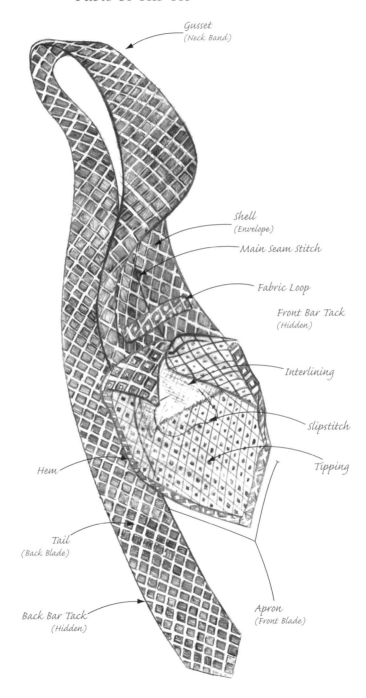

Gusset
(Neck Band)

Shell
(Envelope)

Main Seam Stitch

Fabric Loop

Front Bar Tack
(Hidden)

Interlining

Slipstitch

Hem

Tipping

Tail
(Back Blade)

Back Bar Tack
(Hidden)

Apron
(Front Blade)

## Tie Length

A man's tie should come down to the top of his belt buckle. To accommodate men of different heights, or those who may be long- or short-waisted, ties come in "Regular" for the tie running 56"–57" long, and "Tall" for the tie 60"–61" long. (Always inquire of the salesperson, as there may be a slight difference in measurement depending on the manufacturer.)

If a man is very short, a skilled tailor can alter the tie by shortening the back blade the desired amount.

*Too Short*                    *Correct Length*

## Tie Width

A tie of the correct width is often the most challenging aspect when shopping. Customers are often concerned over whether the width they have selected is "in." Relax. Although the beginning of the 1960s did bring us the infamous string tie with a width of less then an inch, and in the early 1970s some adventurous men flirted with a tie of 5 to 6 inches, in recent years ties have fallen comfortably into the range of 3–4 inches at their widest point.

Proportion, not the "in" width, should be your main concern. Remember, a short man will always look better in a narrow tie, because it will go with his narrower shoulders. (Narrow shoulders mean narrow lapels, and with narrow lapels, the tie must also be narrow.) If you are shopping together, don't let him become distracted by the width that seems popular that particular season. If you buy a tie proportionate to his size, and keep quality construction in mind, you will have a good tie for many years to come.

*Too Narrow*                    *Correct Width*

# Recognizing Quality

No matter what size or pattern tie you select, you want the best quality you can afford. Here are some ways to determine how well a tie has been made:

1 Check that the tie material has been cut on a bias. You can accomplish this by taking hold of the tie by its tail and letting it hang loosely. If it twists instead of hanging straight, it is not cut on the bias.

2 See that the tie's various layers lay smoothly one on top of the other without any perceptible ripples. (Spread it out on a counter to check.)

3 See that the tips at both ends of the tie are cut symmetrically on either side of their center points.

4 Make sure the finished hem at the bottom edge of the apron and the tail of the tie are hand-rolled, not machine-stitched. This rolled edge gives the tie a softer edge and a superior shape.

5 Look for that all-important slipstitch, visible just inside the shell. If you cannot see it, inquire of your salesperson where to find it.

6 Check as a sign of the highest quality workmanship that the pattern on the outside envelope of the tie matches exactly along the joining seam on the back

7 Examine whether the turned back lining lies equidistant from the edges of the tie all around the back of the apron and tail.

8 And lastly, be aware that the best made tie will most likely have the maker's name woven, rather than printed, into the fabric.

*"Women play a crucial role in the world of men's ties. Because they advise their husbands, and offer them ties as gifts, wives have a powerful influence on tie fashions."*

*Francois Chaille*

# Tie Textures

The weight, feel, and texture of material are referred to as the "hand." Here is a primer on the types of materials used to make ties.

## Sensuous silk

A 100 percent silk tie is the "Cadillac" of ties, as it is considered to be of the highest quality "hand." Not only does a silk tie look beautiful, it also holds a knot more securely than any other tie material. The highest-quality silk ties are woven with thread that has already been dyed to the color and pattern of the tie. Since the 1960s, however, better dying techniques have permitted piece-dying, meaning the pattern is printed onto the silk after it is woven. The results are equally successful and are found at more modest prices.

Although silk is always desirable, not all silks are the same. Specifically, there are several classifications of silk associated with tie-making.

a  "Raw silk," most often imported from China, comes primarily in the form of twill (characterized by diagonal ribbing).

b  "Gum twill," a lightweight silk with a more open weave is popular for summer wear (along with cotton), and is widely known for its velvety touch.

c  "Crepe de chine," another better-known silk, is noted by its shiny, finely-twisted threads, and wrinkly texture.

d  "Grosgrain," a heavyweight silk with horizontal round ribbing and a dull sheen, is more commonly associated with little girl's hair ribbons.

## Silk blends

These are also popular, and include "Irish poplin," a silk blended with an equal amount of wool. Originating with the silk weavers of Avignon, France, who fled north to escape religious persecution during the 1600s, this Irish poplin fabric with its corded texture makes a rich and firmly constructed tie.

## Wool

A very interesting alternative to the all-silk or blended-silk tie is the 100 percent wool tie, or one made of wool blended with cashmere or alpaca. This tie, with its own brand of autumn richness and texture, adds luster to the simplest gray flannel suit or casual sports jacket.

# Patterns

Although ties are usually displayed in a dizzying myriad of patterns and colors, each can be considered a member or variation on one of the following eight categories. Learn the types of tie that are the most versatile or appropriate for your man's lifestyle.

## Something Solid

Versatility is the name of the game when it comes to a solid tie. Solids move easily from dressy to casual without a second thought. A solid tie takes its character and appropriateness from the color and weight of the threads in its weave. Navy blue, burgundy, and brown are the most popular colors for solid ties. Bright reds denote a confrontation. Black ties are worn exclusively for formal occasions. Even for a funeral, a man should choose a "quiet" navy, rather than a black tie.

## The Regimental Tie

The worst kept secret in the world of ties is the classic striped or "regimental tie." Far and above the most recognizable pattern, it is also the best-selling tie in the world. The tradition of wearing a striped tie first began in Britain in the 1920s, when various military regiments and popular fraternal organizations began selling their members ties with numerous stripes representing the group's traditional colors. Wearing such a tie brought a man status and identity. The striped tie of today still features diagonal stripes running from the upper left shoulder to the lower right hand of the wearer in the British version, and from the upper right shoulder to lower left hand in the American.

## The University Tie

There is a slight difference between what is known as the "regimental tie," and its brother, the "university tie." While the regimental tie has a solid background with two or three alternating bands of color running across it, the university tie has only two bands of color of equal width running across the tie, with no background color at all.

Membership in any particular group is no longer a prerequisite for wearing either a regimental or a university tie. They both come in every color combination that your man or any designer could possibly imagine.

Striped ties are popular with men for a number of reasons. To begin with, the diagonal stripes running across a man's chest make his body and face look slimmer. Stripes minimize any sweetness in a man's expression, creating that more determined "let's get down to business" look. Striped ties are also less expensive to manufacture than ties in more complicated patterns, thus you can get a great look for a reasonable price. Lastly, they lend a clean, crisp look, consistent with traditional suits and dress shirt combinations.

## The Foulard

A foulard tie is any tie featuring an even pattern of small geometric or abstract shapes that cover the entire body of the tie. There is no limit on the creativity of these patterns. This motif was first introduced to America in 1890 by the Madison Avenue men's shop, Brooks Brothers.

## Polka Dot

Dots were the first printed design ever to appear on men's ties. You will easily identify this pattern as a set of four small dots arranged around a fifth, center dot. Polka dots come across the liveliest when combined with a pin- or chalk-striped suit.

## Paisleys

The Paisley pattern typically includes abstract, elongated, curved shapes and intricate swirls. It can be found on both woven and printed ties. Although traditionally associated with shawls first made during Victorian times in the town of Paisley, Scotland, the very roots of this pattern go back to designs of ancient Babylon. The Paisley was adapted for men's ties during the 1920s, and, because of its British, Ivy League look, it is often described as the "fun tie" for men of the upper crust.

## Plaids and Tartans

A plaid pattern, including the Scottish tartan, consists of many lines of varying widths crossing others at right angles to form boxes of different shapes and sizes. Found in both woven and printed ties, this pattern had its origin not around the neck, but over the shoulder in blankets used by Scottish Highland sheepherders to ward off the cold. These box designs come in many, often bold, color combinations, which still identify historical Scottish clans. Plaids are favored by men with Scottish roots or propensity, as well as by men who appreciate the richness of a plaid's color and design.

## Sports and Club Ties

These specialized ties, much like the regimental tie, originated in the "for members only" clubs of Great Britain. Their repetitive pattern is created with small symbols relating to the sport most associated with the club. Variations include tiny boating flags, golf tees, or tennis racquets. My son, Peter, who is in the film business, received as a present a club tie designed with miniature movie cameras. Hermes, the world famous maker of silk scarves and ties, may be recognized by its own equestrian design.

Sports or club ties should only be worn for casual occasions, and never at the office or similar environment.

# Pattern Categories

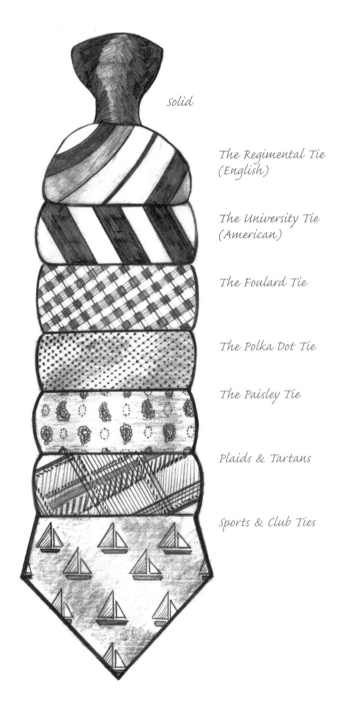

Solid

The Regimental Tie
(English)

The University Tie
(American)

The Foulard Tie

The Polka Dot Tie

The Paisley Tie

Plaids & Tartans

Sports & Club Ties

# The Tie That Binds: Knots

After seeing the 1977 Woody Allen film "Annie Hall," the Diane Keaton character influenced me to experiment with wearing men's ties. I used to steal all the ties ignored or discarded by my husband. This later served me well when it came time for teaching my growing son how to tie his own "four-in-hand," and for assisting my husband with his less frequently worn formal bow tie. Today, women wearing men's ties has pretty much gone out of style, reducing the chance that many women will have any knowledge about various types of knots and how to create them.

The three most popular knots for men's ties include:

1 **The Full Windsor.** This is the largest, most bulky knot and requires extra loops for its execution. The larger man with broad shoulders and broad lapels, who wears a spread shirt collar should choose this knot.

2 **The Half-Windsor.** This knot is smaller and therefore less bulky than the Full Windsor. For that reason, it is more popular with the average-size man.

3 **The Four-In-Hand.** This knot, referred to as the "slip knot," or "sailor's knot," is the most popular knot of all. It is also the least complicated. It has a clean look, ties easily with any fabric, and results in dimensions which fit comfortably between the points of any soft, turn down, or dress shirt collar.

As a rule-of-thumb, the knot of a tie should always rest as high as possible into the inverted V of the two points of the shirt collar. This creates a small inverted pleat in the tie just beneath the knot itself. The knot should be loose enough to be comfortable, but tight enough to make the tie stand out from the shirt collar. This produces a pulled-together business look.

# High Flying–Bow Ties

When buying a bow tie for him, you will find they come in three classic shapes with some rather eccentric names.

1 **The Butterfly,** named after the opera "Madame Butterfly" when first performed in the year 1904, is still the most popular bow tie for men. Often referred to as a "thistle" or "papillon". it flares broadly from the center knot to a width between 2¼ to 3¾ inches. When displayed, untied, it has a bubble shape and flat vertical ends. When worn, it exhibits a slight curve at the bottom and top of the flair.

2 **The "Diamond Point" Butterfly** has the same bubble shape except that its tips are pointed instead of having a flat vertical cut.

3 **The Bat Wing** has vertical side wings measuring 1½ to 2 inches in overall width, and is easily recognized by having a straight cut rather than a bubble shape.

## Bow Ties–Three Classic Shapes

The Butterfly

The Diamond Point

The Bat Wing

# How To Tie The Full-Windsor Knot
## (While he is looking in the mirror)

**Step One:** To begin with, the apron of the tie should be on his right extending down approximately 12 inches longer than the tail.

**Step Two:** Wrap the longer apron around the shorter tail from the front to the back and pull it up through the loop from the back to the front with the apron finishing up on the left side.

**Step Three:** Bring the longer apron down and wrap it behind the shorter tail finishing up on the right side.

**Step Four:** Thread the longer apron through the loop from the front to the back pulling down and wrapping it across the front of the knot from the left to the right.

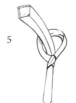

**Step Five:** Pull the apron through the loop again.

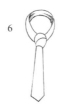

**Step Six:** Now slip the apron point through the front of the knot and tighten the knot by pulling down on the tail with one hand while sliding the knot into place with the other.

# How To Tie The Half-Windsor Knot
## (While he is looking in the mirror)

 1    **Step One:** To begin with, the apron of the tie should be on his right extending down approximately 12 inches longer than the tail.

 2    **Step Two:** Wrap the longer apron around the shorter tail from the front to the back with the apron finishing up on the right side.

 3    **Step Three:** Thread the longer apron through the loop from the front to the back and pull it down toward the left.

 4    **Step Four:** Cross the apron over in front of the knot from the left to the right.

 5    **Step Five:** Pull the apron through the loop from the back to the front.

 6    **Step Six:** Now slip the apron point through the front of the knot and tighten the knot by pulling down on the tail with one hand while sliding the knot into place with the other.

# How To Tie The Four-In Hand Knot
## (While he is looking in the mirror)

1  **Step One:** To begin with, the apron of the tie should be on his right extending down approximately 12 inches longer than the tail.

2  **Step Two:** Wrap the longer apron around the shorter tail from the front to the back with the apron finishing up on the right side.

3  **Step Three:** Continue to cross the longer apron over the shorter tail finishing up on the left side.

4  **Step Four:** Thread the longer apron through the loop from the back.

5  **Step Five:** Slip the apron point through the front of the knot and tighten.

6  **Step Six:** While pulling down on the tail with one hand slide the knot into place with the other.

# How To Tie A Bow Tie
## (While he is looking in the mirror)

**Step One:** To begin with, the left end of the tie should extend 1 /2 inches longer than the right end.

**Step Two:** Cross the longer left end over the shorter right end pulling the longer end through the loop form the back to the front; then pull it tight.

**Step Three:** Fold the remaining short end so as to form the front loop of the bow.

**Step Four:** Secure the front loop with the thumb and the forefinger of left hand and let the long end droop down over the front center of the loop.

**Step Five:** Loop the long end around the right forefinger pointing up.

**Step Six:** Now push the new loop through the knot behind the first loop.

**Step Seven:** Pull tightly and adjust the two sides until they are even.

## Again, Size Counts

There are two considerations when you are choosing a bow tie. The first is the length. A bow tie, when tied correctly, should never be wider than the wearer's face. The second is the width: the tie should not be wider than his dress shirt collar. If his bow tie is too large, it will make him look like a clown. If it is too small, it will make his head look oversized.

Bow ties come in either neck sizes or are designed to be adjustable. They can be altered if too long. It is advisable to try on a bow tie before purchase. Check with the in-house tailor if you have any concerns about its size or length.

## Advantages and Disadvantages of the Bow Tie

When purchasing a bow tie for him, keep in mind its tendency to attract attention. If your man is normally a low-profile personality, wearing a bow tie in the office may create more of a stir than he is comfortable with. There are a number of professions, however, where a bow tie is an asset. Men who work bent over a drawing board, for example, may find a bow tie to be highly practical.

One final thought: advise the man in your life to avoid clip-on bow ties; clip-ons are considered unsophisticated. Yes, it is more difficult to tie a standard bow tie than to clip one on, but it is no harder than learning to tie your shoe.

## The Ascot

An Ascot is a very wide, unlined tie featuring two aprons of equal size connected by a narrow pleated center strip. Its origin dates back to England in the 1770s where British noblemen created the style at the annual running of the horses at the Ascot-Heath race course. Presently, Ascots, created in similar patterns and materials as neckties, can be worn tucked under the open collar of an oxford casual shirt, a rolled-neck sweater, or an outer wool jacket. An Ascot adds flash to any everyday outfit, but it is often associated with formal daytime weddings where the two wide ends of the Ascot are crossed one over the other and held together with a decorative gold or mother-of-pearl tie pin.

# 14

# Mixing & Matching

*"Women tend to be better than men at rapidly identifying matching items, a skill called perceptual speed."*

*Doreen Kimura*

When your man stands frozen in front of his closet, he may be trying to decide what to wear with what. The easiest way to help him get unstuck is to have him select his foundation piece. This core garment is either a complete suit or a sports jacket paired with trousers. This first decision will dictate the colors, patterns, textures and fabrics for his entire ensemble.

Next you should move on to his dress shirt, which will set off his suit (or sports jacket/trousers); and then on to his tie, which will complement every piece chosen previously. Finally, you will choose the color and style of his shoes, belt, socks, and pocket square.

## Combining Solid Colors

Chapter 2 discusses the importance of recognizing his best color range and degrees of contrast based on his skin tones, hair and eye color. How to coordinate these colors in an outfit is the focus of this section. Beginning with how to combine solids, which may sound a bit dull, the look can be smart and sophisticated when done well.

### Color Safe

The safest ensemble in solid colors is to combine three solids–one for his suit, one for his shirt, one for his tie. The most popular grouping is a navy blue suit, a white dress shirt, and a red tie. This classic trio has a clean look with striking contrasts. A red tie–in a shade that honors his coloring–also denotes (as noted previously) an assertive demeanor essential for important meetings and public appearances.

*" When in doubt, wear red."*

*Bill Blass*

(Hint: Your man should never wear a solid navy tie with a solid navy suit. All colors of navy are not the same, and will seldom match. Also, a navy suit and tie will give the impression of a uniform.)

## The Strongest Statement

If you decide to mix three solid colors, bear in mind that his suit color will always dominate. To achieve a classic look, his jackets, trousers, and suits should be selected in dark or muted shades, his shirts and ties adding the brighter accents. Dress shirts in white, beige or pale blue provide neutral backdrops for his ties.

If your man is drawn to brighter colors, the pastel dress shirt has become highly acceptable in addition to the classic white for office wear. However, only in tropical climates can pastel colors be considered appropriate for sports jackets and business suits.

## Two From the Same Family

When combining three solid colors (other than white) two of the solids should belong to the same color family. If the suit is navy, a soft blue dress shirt will look best, with the tie providing the addition of a third color. If the suit is dark to medium brown a beige shirt should be selected, with the tie again introducing the third color. A light blue shirt under a navy blue blazer will also do nicely with gray slacks if a tie or pocket square is not included.

It bears repeating that navy is the one suit color that will lend itself to any combination of dress shirt and tie. This applies to all men, no matter what their personal color range.

When building a wardrobe from scratch, make the first suit a navy blue, the second a charcoal or medium gray. By adding a light blue dress shirt, he will be able to wear most any color tie with either of these combinations.

## The Color Message of Tweed

A tweed suit or sports jacket, due to its tight weave, can be treated as a solid color even though it is composed of a number of subtle colors. Discern the dominant color of the tweed and work with that when choosing trousers and shirt.

Bear in mind that if a sports coat is removed during a casual occasion, the trousers have to work well with the shirt and tie. Double-check how he looks jacket-less before letting him out the door!

## Matching With Lines or Flecks of Color

Closely examine the color of the suit you have chosen. Although it might appear a plain black, navy, charcoal, or brown at first, there are actually barely perceptible lines or flecks in the material that make the suit unique. These tiny threads will influence the shade of the overall color to help in matching it with other parts of the outfit.

Look closely at these colors and carry them over into his shirt and tie. If a suit is not solid but a true weave, and the colors are very close within a specific range, a tie that features a highly contrasting solid color can be worn. For example, a brown/rust flecked suit combines well with a warm green tie.

### The Dress Shirt and Tie Link

The dress shirt can provide the foundation to harmonize or set off the tie. For example, the tie can establish a monochromatic theme, such as a beige shirt with a rust tie, or liven up a dark, neutral suit with contrast by pairing a muted green shirt with a red tie.

## Patterns in the Mix

Here are some tips for classic coordination of solids and patterns:

### Tried and True, Navy Blue

Combining a navy suit with a striped tie–with one stripe matching the navy of the suit– is very effective.

### When Two Is Too Much

The color you are carrying over from one piece to the next should never appear again more than once. For example, picking up a red fleck from a navy suit in a pink and red pin-striped dress shirt is okay, but not if you add a solid red tie. A better choice would be the same suit with a soft gray dress shirt, and a red and gray striped tie. Here the tie would bring out the red fleck in the navy suit, while picking up the soft gray of the dress shirt with no color repeated more than twice.

### The Darker Dress Shirt

Shirts in dark colors have recently, perhaps for their slimming effect, become very popular with men. A dark shirt–chocolate brown, midnight blue, maroon, black–will look best with a solid knit or muted patterned tie. Steer him away, however, from wearing his dark shirt with a very light colored tie and using the full Windsor knot. Historically, this combination is associated with Al Capone and other gangsters of the 1920s!

### The Pocket Pet

If adding a pocket square or handkerchief, refer to the color and pattern of his tie to determine the best color for this accent. Good style does not permit, however, that the pocket square and tie match exactly. (See Chapter 20 for a full discussion of pocket squares.)

# Combining Patterns

Englishmen have always had a flair for combining patterns. In the 1920s, the Prince of Wales pushed the envelope of taste by creatively mixing checks, stripes, and plaids–all in the same outfit.

Since the man in your life is also a prince of sorts, let me share a few principles that you must keep in mind when tackling the problem of combining patterns.

• Patterns should work together harmoniously, and should never fight one another. As a general rule, the larger the personality, the larger or bolder the pattern.

• The more subtle the combination of color, pattern, and texture, the more dressy the outfit looks. The more bold the combination, the more casual.

• Dotted ties are extremely versatile and can be combined easily with pin or chalk striped suits, as well as an endless number of dress shirts.

• Checked shirts are generally considered to be casual. However, the smaller the check, the dressier the shirt. When mixing a checked tie with a checked shirt, the tie should be the bolder of the two either in the larger size of the checks or in the dominance of their color.

Here are some specific how-to's:

1  If you want to combine two stripes, the contrast in the size of the patterns must be pronounced, while the color themes remain close. For example, combine a pinstriped shirt in soft blue and white with a very wide striped tie in navy and medium blue. Similarly, a narrow striped dress shirt can be combined with a wide chalk striped navy or charcoal suit. The same goes for checks, although they are a little trickier. A tie with a very small checked pattern will coordinate beautifully with a dress shirt containing a large check so long as the colors in the tie dominate and they both share at least one color in common.

2  For two totally different patterns such as a stripe and a check to work together, select patterns of the same proportion. For example, a large checked sports jacket will go well with an equally prominent tie with wide stripes. Exception: if one of the patterns is exceedingly small, the other must be much larger. Two very small but different patterns, when placed side by side, are far too busy.

3  To give your man more confidence when combining patterns, encourage him to select a solid colored shirt as a neutral area for separating patterns. With a solid space as a go-between, a tweed suit in a small check, a glen plaid, or a rich herringbone can be combined beautifully with a bold striped tie.

4  Contrasting patterns, which fall within the same color range, are very appealing. A paisley, foulard, or club tie will work equally well with a pinstripe suit or a plaid jacket, as long as the colors in one piece are closely repeated in the other.

# Combining Patterns Successfully

Tweed suit, white shirt & striped tie (Using white as a neutral dividing area)

Chalk striped suit, striped shirt & solid tie (Combining two stripes - one large & one small)

Herringbone suit, checked shirt & foulard tie (Combining three different patterns - all the same scale)

# A Potpourri of Three

**A ménage-à-trois:** Some gurus in the world of men's attire believe combining three or more patterns is out of the question. They believe in such a case the clothes are wearing the man rather than the reverse. I disagree.

When you have gained confidence combining two patterns, you will feel more comfortable combining three. Three different patterns all of the same scale will combine most effectively, such as a herringbone sports jacket with a striped shirt and a foulard tie.

If you are going to combine three plaids or three stripes, you are going to revert to the rule on combining two of the same pattern: the contrast in the size of the patterns must be pronounced, while the color themes remain close. For example, you might combine successfully, here, a medium striped shirt in white and purple with a navy chalk striped suit, while adding an even larger striped tie, mirroring both the colors in the shirt and the suit.

You might also combine two of the same pattern with the inclusion of a dissimilar third. You could, for example, combine two stripes of different scales with a check. Here the check would have to blend well with the more dominant of the two stripes. One solution would be to combine a large checked sports jacket, a small checked dress shirt and a large boldly striped tie in the predominant colors of the jacket.

## Or Even Four!

To mix four patterns, each should be subtle. You could combine two different checks, one large in the sports jacket and one small in the tie. Then add a shirt with a stripe, and a foulard (a small geometric design) pocket square. The mixing of this number of patterns relies heavily on the mirroring of colors throughout the various patterns to keep them linked.

*"Style is a simple way of saying complicated things."*

*Jean Cocteau*

## Combining Textures

Bringing together different textures in an outfit will suggest a level of informality or formality. For example, a man dressed in a tweed jacket with an oxford shirt and solid textured tie is ready for a casual walk in the country; whereas the man in a buttery wool suit, a Sea Island cotton dress shirt, and silk foulard tie paints a picture of a fast- paced evening on the town. In general, coarse or raised textures (such as tweeds, oxford cloth, loose knits, corduroy, denim) go casual; smooth or supple fabrics (tight knits, cashmere, gabardine, fine wools, silk) convey elegance in business or evening wear.

When combining textures, keep seasonality consistent. It is inappropriate to wear a winter-weight jacket with a summer shirt. For example, a light summer suit will look best with a cotton tie, not a heavy silk one. A summer suit also takes a linen handkerchief. Heavy winter tweed jackets and flannel slacks need a woolen tie and a cashmere pocket square. Remember that in men's clothing, wool isn't always for winter. Woolens with a weight of 12 ounces per square yard are considered winter weight. Other thinner woolens have a lighter year-round weight of 8 to 10 ounces.

## When in Doubt–Don't

It makes little difference whether you are mixing colors, patterns or textures–if he is undecided about a combination, suggest another. The skill of combining items will improve as you both gain experience. Once successful selections have been made, you will begin to trust your eye and can venture forth into more daring combinations, as you are inclined. There is a fine line between an exciting combination and one that doesn't work. Be patient. The time you give to skillful "mixing and matching" will be richly rewarded by the compliments he receives.

# Combining Solids, Patterns & Textures

| Components | Rules | Example |
|---|---|---|
| 3 SOLIDS | Two of the solids should reside in the same color family. The third color should depart from the theme. | Navy suit, medium or light blue shirt, red tie.<br>*The suit makes the strongest statement. The shirt is the backdrop. The tie is the focal point.* |
| 2 LIKE PATTERNS | Two patterns, which are the same, must be vastly different in size. The dissimilar third must blend in color with the most dominant of the other patterns. | A large checked sports jacket in brown and rust, a small striped shirt in eggshell and light brown and a wide striped university tie in orange and rust.<br>*Note: The patterned tie must always be bolder than the shirt.* |
| 2 UNLIKE PATTERNS | The patterns should echo colors found in each. The pattern proportions should be the same.<br>*Exception: Two very small patterns look too busy together. In this case make one much larger than the other.* | A solid navy suit, a narrow blue-striped shirt, and a tie with navy and soft blue squares. |
| 3 LIKE PATTERNS | There must be broad contrast in their size with their colors falling into the same family. | Combine a gray pinstripe suit, a small striped mauve shirt, a large striped navy and purple tie, following the parallel rule. |
| 4 UNLIKE PATTERNS | Rely heavily on the mirroring of colors throughout the varying patterns. Subtlety of color and pattern becomes essential. | A checked sports jacket, a dotted tie, a striped shirt and a foulard pocket square. |
| COMBINING – WEIGHTS & TEXTURES | Weights and textures should match within a single outfit.<br>*Exception: A pocket square and tie are most effective when their textures contrast.* | A tweed jacket, an oxford button-down shirt with a solid wool tie. Example 2: A merino suit, Sea Island cotton shirt, and a silk foulard tie with linen pocket square. |

# REMINDERS

**1** Solid neutral color comfortably separates patterns.

**2** Lines should run parallel or nearly parallel in an ensemble.

**3** Subtle combinations of color, pattern, and texture are considered formal.

**4** Bold combinations of color, pattern, and texture are considered casual.

**5** Summer weight and winter weight fabric should not be worn together.

# 15

# Putting His Best Foot Forward

*"Shoes are the first adult machines we are given to master."*

*Nicholson Baker*

## If the Shoe Fits...

No matter how beautiful a pair of shoes may be, there is nothing to rave about if they don't fit well. In the 1940s, X-ray machines were used to help customers select shoes that fit. Fortunately, these machines have been outlawed. Now a customer is on his own to make sure the shoes he tries on will be comfortable inside as well as outside the store, but there are some things you can do to ensure the way a shoe feels when you try it on will feel the same when you get it home.

First, because feet swell during the day, save his shoe buying for the last shopping activity of the day. Shoes that feel fine in the morning may pinch by late afternoon.

Second, because most men have one foot larger than the other, always try on both left and right shoes before buying.

As you may already do upon occasion, to assure that the shoes will match the suit or slacks he will wear them with, and can accommodate the thickness of the intended socks, have him wear both at the time of purchase.

# Categories of Men's Shoes

Men's shoes fall into three basic categories:

1 Shoes that are fastened with laces.
2 Shoes that are fastened with a buckle or buckles.
3 Shoes that slip under and over his foot, commonly referred to as "slip-ons."

Within these categories we find any number of variations. The following descriptions will be handy in identifying versatile, always-in-fashion footwear for men.

# An Oxford Education

Since it was first worn at the famed university in Great Britain in the early 1800s, the oxford lace-up shoe with its rounded toe has been ranked highest for sheer elegance. The two variations on the oxford style give the wearer an option for formal or less formal occasions.

**1 The Balmoral,** the more formal oxford, named after the castle in Scotland frequented by the royal family, has a closed throat lacing displaying generally five pairs of holes. It can be identified by the "quarters" which extend up from the sole on either side of the shoe, overlapping at the tongue. These quarters are sewn into the shoe underneath the "vamp" (the part over the instep where the tongue of the shoe is attached). This style of oxford with its smooth, uninterrupted lines looks especially graceful on any man with a narrow foot, and sets off a pair of cuffed trousers beautifully.

**2 The Derby,** or "bluchers," the less formal oxford, has an open throat lacing. The quarter sidepieces are attached on the outside of the vamp, allowing extra room for inserting the foot and doing up the laces. It is therefore more comfortable for a man with a high instep or a wide foot. The tongue, unlike the Balmoral, is not sewn to the vamp, but is actually an extension of the vamp. The sole is also heavier.

The Derby is versatile and therefore practical. A plain black Derby with a black, dark gray, or navy suit can nearly match the elegance of the Balmoral; yet when purchased in a medium brown, nappy leather or with a rubber sole, will go equally well with a pair of jeans or a sports jacket with corduroy trousers.

"Capping it off" becomes of prime importance when choosing either the Balmoral or the Derby. They are both sold with either a "plain toe cap," a piece of smooth leather lying across the toe, or with a "decorated toe cap," one with brogueing, or "punchings" of various sizes, arranged in decorative designs.

# The Oxford Shoe

**The Balmoral**
*More formal - with closed throat or (V) lacing*

**The Derby (Blucher)**
*Less formal - with open throat lacing*

Farmers in the Scottish Highlands and in Ireland originated the craft of brogueing to allow water to seep out of their shoes after sloshing through a soggy bog. Now strictly decorative, they are carefully placed along the seams of a shoe, or in the upper front portion of the toe. The Prince of Wales first made shoes with brogueing fashionable for city folk in the 1930s.

Oxford shoes are divided into three identifiable sub-styles based on the amount and the arrangement of these punchings, normally ranging in size from ⅛ to ½₅ of an inch across:

1 **The "medallion brogue oxford"**–a plain shoe where only the toecap has been decorated.

2 **The "semi-brogue oxford"**–a shoe that may or may not have decoration over part or all of the double stitching, but will always have a straight-line decoration on the toecap.

3 **The "full-brogue oxford"** or wing-tip: a shoe where the decoration is shaped like a bird with outstretched wings, with further decoration extending along the double-stitched seams from the front cap to the heel of the shoe.

The more brogueing found on a shoe, the more casual it becomes. It is, therefore, inappropriate for a man to wear a shoe with either semi- or full-brogueing after six o'clock in the evening. When an oxford shoe is worn after six, it must be plain and black.

If the man in your life is starting out on a new career and can only afford to buy one pair of quality shoes, make it the Balmoral oxford in black leather with a plain cap. This one pair of shoes will carry him comfortably through his office day into your most enchanted evenings together.

# Oxford Sub-Styles
(Based on the amount and arrangement of the brogueing)

**Medallion Brogue**
*Plain with decoration only on toe*

**Semi-Brogue**
*Straight-line decoration on toe with or without decoration on double stitching*

**Full-Brogue or Wingtip**
*Decoration on toe in the shape of a bird with outstretched wings*

## The Spectacular Spectator

This shoe is my favorite. As a little girl, I thought my grandfather had the most beautiful feet in the world. In the summer, "Ba Ba" wore white suede or calfskin shoes with beige, brown or black trim. They were called "spectators."

The man's two-toned spectator with its Balmoral styling, semi- or full-brogueing, and its sturdy construction has been a popular style for men going back to the 1930s. Although the United States gave "the spectator" its name, it was originally designed for British cricket players. Men have not, however, had a corner on the spectator shoe. Women have always loved its style and versatility.

*The Spectacular Spectator*
*Ba Ba's favorite and mine*

## A Monk Shoe (Outside the Monastery)

The monk shoe got its inspiration from a shoe worn by 15th century Italian monks. It is a favorite with men in creative professions as it exhibits more flash than the more conservative oxford. The monk, characterized by a broad tongue and a leather strap which lies across the vamp, is fastened on the outer side of the shoe with a gold or silver saddle buckle. With its clean lines, the monk works well for business in black calf or pigskin. In brown leather or suede, it works equally well for casual wear. This is a comfortable shoe for a man with a wide foot, a hammertoe, or bunions. It is cut fuller across the front, and the buckle can easily be adjusted to accommodate any instep. As a crossover style, this shoe is a practical addition to your man's wardrobe.

*The Monk*
*Good if your man has a wide foot*

# The Parts of His Shoe

The Balmoral oxford in black leather with a plain toecap.
(If he can only afford to buy one pair of shoes, this is the one to buy.)

Lining

Tongue

Counter

Eyelets

Stitching

Heel

Quarter

Facing

Vamp

Straight (plain) Toecap

Sole    Welt

# Slipping Into Something Comfortable

A "slip-on shoe" is any shoe whose upper portion consists of a solid piece of leather, has a thinner sole, and is devoid of laces. Styles include the loafer, the boat or deck shoe, and the moccasin.

## Pennies From Heaven

The most famous slip–on is the "Weejum," better known as the penny loafer. When I was child, we all wanted to wear the trendy loafer to school. Unfortunately, our practical parents forced us to wear the more supportive "saddle shoe," a gunboat that made our feet look twice their size. Still, we dreamed.

The penny loafer is easily recognized by the diamond-shaped band of leather sewn across the base of the tongue. Customarily, a lucky coin is kept tucked in a slit in the band. In brown this classic shoe has historically been associated with casual wear. More recently, when cut from quality black leather, in a plain version, or one with two florets of leather in place of the diamond, it is finding its way into offices. When shopping for loafers, be sure they fit your man snuggly across the instep, and around the heel. Loafers are known to stretch half a size with use.

## Gucci Loafers

In a class by itself, the Gucci loafer is found in brown leather or black suede. With its "signature" buckle across the vamp, it is as soft and as comfortable as it is expensive. This loafer is a widely recognized status symbol.

## Hitting the Deck

The boat shoe, also referred to as the "Top-Sider," is a favorite with men, especially those who consider the water their personal playground. It is constructed of well-oiled, water-resistant calf leather, has rawhide lacing across the vamp for decoration, as well as a non-slip sole for maneuvering around a boat. This shoe is equally at home on terra firma when paired with khakis or linen trousers.

## Moccasins

The American Indian inspired the moccasin. This shoe has hand-stitched aprons, raised or flat seams running along the side of the shoe from the back to the vamp, and a tassel on top. The more popular version of the moccasin has a "welted sole" (a narrow strip of leather stitched to the upper portion and the edge of the insole) to provide it with more stability. Moccasins are strictly weekend wear.

Penny Loafer or Weejum
The most famous slip-on

Gucci Loafer
A real status symbol

Boat Shoe/Top-sider
Suitable for land or sea

Moccasin
With hand-stitched apron

## Office No-No's

Cowboy boots, rubber-soled shoes, sneakers, and snow boots are not appropriate for the office. If he likes to walk to work in any weather, he should discard his boots for a pair of dress shoes once he has arrived. He can keep a pair stashed in the bottom drawer of his desk or in his office closet.

## Shoe Colors

Shoe colors for men run the gamut from black to varying shades of brown, beige and white, black being the dressiest. After black comes dark brown, and then deep reddish brown as in "cordovan." (Although you will seldom see a cordovan shoe worn with a navy suit in the United States, it is highly acceptable in Europe.) Note that cordovan's tone only improves with age and regular polishing. Tan is even less formal, followed by summer white. Navy shoes–or shoes in any non-neutral color for that matter–so popular with women, have never caught on with men.

## About Leather

The cost of a man's shoe is largely determined by the quality of its leather. Due to its porous nature, leather, which keeps a man's feet cooler longer than synthetics, is the most commonly used material. The upper portion (or "uppers") of a dress shoe is most often cut from kidskin, goat, black box calf, brown willow calf, cordovan (a naturally water resistant leather from inside a horse's hindquarters) and the most highly prized French calf (characterized by its smooth feel and dull shine.)

### Formal Wear

Although a plain, black French calf shoe will always be suitable for any semi-formal situation, patent leather is the most appropriate for formal wear. Made by a complicated process of exposing leather to extensive heat, polishing it profusely, and then applying many coats of lacquer, patent leather is produced from kid, calf, cow or even horsehide.

### Casual Wear

Suede, or "reversed calf," with its tanned and buffed nap, creates a look which goes as well with winter flannel trousers and tweed jackets as it does with lighter colored casual attire. Although sometimes used for shoes, alligator and crocodile hides are considered by most observers to be harmful to these species and downright ostentatious.

*"Wanna know if a guy is well dressed?  Look down."*

*George Frazier*

# How to Recognize Quality Shoes

With so many leathers to choose from, it is quickly evident that the type of leather used for constructing a man's shoe may not be nearly as important as the quality of that leather.

Leather is graded on a scale from one to five, (one being the best). This grade is seldom noted on the shoe. When picking out a shoe for him from the rack, rely on the fact that the finest grades of leather will feel like butter in your hand; the smoother the butter, the better the grade. The shoe should also exhibit a uniform grain, and be flexible yet strong. Its "upper" part as well as its sole, heel, lining and insole should be made of quality leather. If the leather appears overly glossy, it may be an indication that "correcting" was done at the factory to cover up inferior leather.

If the insole and the lining of the shoe are leather, they will more easily absorb perspiration as well as allow a man's foot to better conform to the inside of the shoe, thus making the shoe more comfortable. Where the lining of the shoe meets the inside leather, the fold should be smooth and neat. Any bumps or knots inside the shoe will cause extreme discomfort.

*"Luxury must be comfortable, otherwise it is not luxury."*

*Coco Chanel*

Leather soles will also better absorb shock as a man walks. This can be important on hard city sidewalks. The soles should be light tan in color, and should be stitched onto the shoes, not glued. If the sole appears to have been painted black, beware. This is another sign of poor grade leather.

Look for inconspicuous, uneven, handmade stitches. Hand stitching will provide more elasticity, creating less stress on the leather. This will give the shoe a longer life.

Lastly, before you buy, place one of the shoes on a flat, raised surface. Check that the part of the sole directly underneath the instep is curved. Look to see that the front of the heel rests solidly on the flat surface, while the back of the heel does not. The tip of the shoe should also turn up just a touch. If all of these observations prove positive, you can be assured that he is purchasing a well-constructed product.

## A Day Off for His Shoes

It is never a good idea to wear the same pair of shoes two days in a row. Shoes need time to dry out and breathe. By owning three pairs of dress shoes, your man will have sufficient coverage even with one pair at the local shoe repair. A man with a hefty social schedule and little down time may require five pairs.

## How Many Pairs to Own

Which shoe style to select, and how many pairs to buy, depends largely on where and how he spends his time. If a man works in an office Monday through Friday, and then hangs around the house on weekends, he will need three pairs of dress shoes, and at least one casual pair. If his office is casual, make that one pair of dress, and three pairs of casual (not including sneakers or other athletic or work/hiking shoes.)

# 16

# Sock It to 'Em

*"He may be president, but he still comes home and swipes my socks."*

Joseph P. Kennedy, speaking of son, Jack

When my son was thirteen, I made reservations for dinner at a posh restaurant on Manhattan's Upper East Side to celebrate Christmas Eve. After dinner we would attend a Broadway show. When we arrived at the restaurant and were checking our coats at the door, I happened to look down, only to discover that Peter was not wearing socks. He blithely informed me that socks were decidedly "not cool." Throughout dinner, I was suspended somewhere between total mortification and sublime amusement, careful not to do anything which might draw attention to his sockless feet.

Fashion-wise, socks deserve attention as they have the indispensable role of continuing or accenting the color scheme of any outfit. They can also reveal something about the wearer's personality and, especially on casual occasions, can be used as a vehicle for saying something fun or surprising.

## No Problem Sizing

Because sock sizes are universal you need not concern yourself with their country of origin. The size of his socks will correspond to 1½ size larger than the American size of his shoe. If he wears size 10 shoes, his sock size will be 11½. The range of men's sock sizes falls between 9½ and 15. If the tag says "one size fits all" then a man whose shoe size ranges from 8½ to 10½ will be able to wear them. Socks will shrink one-half size when laundered. If your man is muscular and has a heavier calf, choose a larger size.

## Four Lengths

When you are shopping for socks, you will discover that there are four lengths from which to choose. These lengths include:

1 **Short socks** (15cm) which are worn for active sports and exercise.

2 **Ankle socks** (29cm) which are ribbed and can be worn rolled over with men's regular or Bermuda shorts.

3 **Calf-length socks** (38cm) which are worn with business suits, casual trousers, and with more formal attire (when supported by garters.)

4 **Knee socks** (50cm or more) which, for those who prefer them, can be worn with business casual, and formal wear.

Both formal and informal occasions warrant coverage of the area between his trouser hem and the top of his shoes. It is distracting to see skin and hair peeking out from between the top of his socks and the bottom of his trousers when his legs are crossed, whether in a conference room or a party on Saturday night.

## About Sock Materials

Socks are woven from many materials, including:

a **Silk:** Silk socks are extremely strong, and because they don't hold heat, keep feet cool. However, they don't absorb perspiration well.

b **Cashmere:** Cashmere socks are good for warmth and their looks, but won't hold up well over time.

c **Wool:** Wool socks, especially Merino wool, are the best socks you can buy for warmth, absorption, and practicality.

d **Cotton:** Cotton socks are the workhorse of socks. When tightly woven, they are warm, longwearing, and will absorb perspiration readily.

e **Nylon:** Nylon socks, combined with natural fibers, (depending on the mix) provide lightness of weight, warmth, color retention and good absorption of perspiration—with the delightful reputation of never having to be darned.

## Appropriate Colors

The color of socks should always extend the color of his trousers in order to continue the unbroken line of color from his trouser leg to his shoe. The only contradiction to this rule is a light tan trouser. In this instance he should mirror the color of his dark brown shoe.

Black, navy, and charcoal are the best colors for dress socks, with dark brown taking the spotlight for casual occasions. If your man likes the idea of incorporating color into his socks, he should select a muted version of the color already exhibited in his tie, his pocket-square, or his dress shirt.

# Weaves and Textures

As important as choosing the right length and color is paying attention to the weave and texture of socks. Each type says something different about the outfit and the occasion.

a **A plain, flat weave** is the most conservative, yet most versatile sock.

b **A raised rib** comes in many widths. If narrow, the sock is formal. If wider, it is casual.

c **A braided cord** creates ornament in the weave. The thicker the braid, the more sporty the sock.

d **A cable pattern** woven throughout the fabric means the sock can be worn with a suit, but only if the sock is woven of a very thin material. Cable socks as a rule go better with casual wear.

For texture, your best bet is to choose one consistent with the weight of the trouser, jacket and/or sweater. If there is flannel or tweed in his outfit, choose heavier socks to create unity. Conversely, if he is in formal attire, the hose must be of a finer and sheerer variety, with or without a design in the weave.

## Weaves and Textures

*Plain*
*Flat-weave*

*Raised Rib*
*Woven into weave*

*Braided Cord*
*Ornament in weave*

*Cable*
*Woven throughout fabric*

# Major Sock Patterns

Herringbone

Bird's Eye

Dot

Argyle

Clock Pattern

## The Importance of Pattern

Socks with herringbone, bird's-eye, or dot patterns work well when combined with a solid suit. They bring something "unexpected" to an otherwise predictable outfit.

The clock pattern is a subtle line of embellishment created by silk thread which runs down the side of the sock. Your man can wear this sock to extend an already existing stripe as is found, for example, in a pin- or chalk-striped suit.

The Argyle, with its bold diamond pattern that comes in many different color combinations, is one of the more familiar patterns for casual socks. While it is still a classic pattern, it adds a mischievous touch.

## Seeking Out the Best Quality

Here are some things to consider when looking for good quality socks:

a  The finest quality socks will be soft to the touch.
b  Good socks exhibit clean and decisive color.
c  The seam across the tip of the toes will lay flat, avoiding discomfort when worn.
d  Woolen blends with 15 percent or less nylon will give him the luxurious look and feel he desires while providing him with durability.

To further extend the life of his socks, always buy them in bulk. As my friend Josephine tells me, "My husband has one brand of socks that he likes, so I wait for the annual Gold Toe sock sale and buy a box of each of the dark colors in the over-the-calf style that he prefers." At a minimum, buy three pairs of the same socks, as one will inevitably get separated in the wash, and having the extra two pairs will provide him with more than three times the longevity.

# 17

# Keeping Up Appearances

## Suspenders

Suspenders create the illusion of wide shoulders and a narrow waist. Thus, the man who wears suspenders radiates health, wealth, power, and position. Just ask the concierge at any five-star hotel who is in a position to observe how men of influence dress.

The French invented this ingenious method for keeping trousers from sliding off the waist. As it turns out, pleated suit trousers hang more gracefully with suspenders than they do with a belt. When creating a custom suit, (unless instructed to the contrary by the client), tailors will include six buttons on the waistband for attaching suspenders. The correct placement of these buttons is between the side pocket and the dominant front pleat, and on either side of the center seam in back. This arrangement provides the ideal tension and location to keep the suspenders from slipping off the shoulders.

## Design and Construction

Suspenders extend from the waistband on the front of the trousers, curve over the shoulders, converge at the shoulder blades, and continue as a single band down the middle of the back to the waistband. Presently, the finest quality suspenders are fashioned from rayon with buckskin fittings, although in the past they were often made up in silk or satin. Each band is generally from 1¼ to 1½ inches wide. The bands attach to the waistband, both in front and in back, with looped catgut braces. These braces fasten onto buttons generally sewn on the inside of the waistband so that the trousers can be worn without a vest. (Trousers designed for suspenders do not have loops fashioned for a belt.)

Suspenders normally come in only one size, with adjustment levers to accommodate long- and short-waisted men. These levers, generally made of brass, rest below his ribs so as not to appear bulky when wearing a vest. If your man is extremely short-waisted, his suspenders can be shortened by a tailor, or even by a local shoe repair shop. If your man is extremely long-waisted, you will on occasion find suspenders that come in extra-long.

*"It is a bad plan that admits no modification."*

*Publitius Syrus*

A single band runs down the middle of his back

Brass levers lie between the breast area and the waist

Looped braces, in back and front.

## Comfort-ability

It might seem that suspenders would be uncomfortable in hot weather, but that is not so. Suspenders keep a man cooler than a belt because they allow air to circulate freely about his body.

## Considerations

Suspenders come in solids, patterns and stripes which are normally woven directly into the fabric. Because both his tie and suspenders are prominently displayed when a jacket or vest is removed, coordination of these two items should be carefully considered. Unity between tie and suspenders can be accomplished by carrying over a single color from one to the other.

While some men wear suspenders daily, they are always the tasteful choice for more formal occasions. You may see clip-on suspenders for sale in men's shops, but they cannot match the elegance of the button-on variety.

A hard and fast rule: Suspenders and a belt should never be worn together.

# The Belt

Belts, which in the 1920s gained wide acceptance in America as a replacement for suspenders, can also confer status. Perhaps this is because the belt echoes the girding of men in preparation for battle. We catch a glimpse of this association today with the way a triumphal prize fighter struts around the ring after a knockout holding up his championship belt.

## Sizing

When buying a belt, always select one size larger than the waist measurement of his trousers because belts run smaller than trouser waist sizes. To check its fit, see that your man can buckle it at the second hole with the tip of the belt coming to a point half way between the first and second loop.

## The Best Materials and Styles

For dressy occasions, a belt should be constructed both inside and out with a quality grade of leather, preferably calfskin. Although snakeskin, lizard, crocodile, and alligator may provide interesting grain patterns, be careful to keep such belts low key. All dress belts should exhibit small, simple buckles in either silver or gold, so as not to draw undo attention to his stomach. If he is wearing a monk shoe, the buckle of the shoe should match the finish on the buckle of his belt. The most versatile width for a belt to be worn with a business suit is between 1¼ to 1½ inches.

Belts for casual wear can be wider, thicker, and made up in any number of materials including woven leather, suede or canvas. The buckle on a casual belt can be more flamboyant. If he is wearing a suede shoe, his belt should also be suede. Wide, carved, leather cowboy belts with flashy oversized buckles should be relegated to vacations on Montana dude ranches.

## Color Coordination

The color of his belt can enhance an ensemble enormously. Make sure the color of his shoes and belt are similar, and that they set off the color of his jacket and trousers. His belt should also be a shade darker than his suit. The darker the belt, the dressier it becomes. The greater the difference in color between his belt and his suit or trousers, the more casual the outfit will become.

Every man should own a belt in black, brown, and cordovan. A reversible belt with black on one side and brown on the other will cut this requirement to two. Once his basic dress belts have been purchased, he can move on to the lighter colored, heavier woven or canvas styles we have previously discussed.

.

# 18

# Pocket Square? No Way!

*"A plain white handkerchief is the sure sign of a confident and elegant dresser."*

*Alan Flusser, designer and author*

## A Touch of the Past and the Present

Some people associate pocket squares with the Roaring Twenties. Although very popular then, they did fade from fashion for a time. Now, they are back. A well-positioned pocket square–though totally inappropriate for blowing one's nose–adds romance and panache to the plainest of jackets.

## A Pocket Square or a Handkerchief?

Pocket squares and handkerchiefs are basically the same item, a pocket square having evolved away from functionality to become an accessory only. So, if you are looking for a decorative handkerchief in a silk or silk blend, you will have to ask your salesperson for a pocket square. Pocket squares are normally 16 to 18 inch squares and can also be purchased in wool, wool blends or cashmere.

If you are looking for handkerchiefs for practical, not decorative, use, you will mostly likely be shown a box of the best quality "lawn" linen white handkerchiefs. A less expensive combination of cotton and linen has a similar look, and is equally durable through many launderings.

Remember that a good handkerchief can be used as a pocket square as it will stay crisp.

Whether choosing a pocket square or a handkerchief, check for quality by seeing that the hem is rolled, not pressed, and that the stitches are done by hand.

# Palettes and Patterns

A pocket square and a tie should never match exactly in color or pattern, no matter how many boxed sets you find in shops over the holidays. Not only should they not match, they should be of different fabrics.

A pocket square is most effective as an accent when it contains one color found in his shirt and another found in his tie. For example, your man might combine a navy suit, with a blue-striped dress shirt, a red tie and a silk pocket square in a foulard pattern with one of the blues found in either the suit or the shirt and the same red found in the tie.

Historically, a pocket square was considered to be a mark of formality and was therefore seldom seen without a tie. That custom has changed. A pocket square presently is as likely to be seen without a tie as with one. In such a case colors to carry over must be found in his shirt, vest, or suit.

## Combining Weights

In addition to color, the weight of the materials must also be considered when choosing a pocket square. A wool or cashmere square will go better with a heavy tweed jacket than will a sheer white linen handkerchief, which would combine well with a fine merino wool business suit.

## Presentation

No matter how it is folded, a pocket square or handkerchief should look relaxed and unstructured. Here are a few traditional methods for folding a pocket square:

### The Television or Square End Fold

This fold, made popular by television personalities of the 1940s and 50s, as well as by President Harry S. Truman, is good for the novice as it is easy and works for any fabric. Fold the square so that a finished straight edge of material is exposed ½ inch above and parallel to the pocket's rim. This fold looks especially sharp on a dark suit and a white or soft blue cotton dress shirt. In white linen or cotton, it adds a touch of savoir-faire without advertising itself.

*Television or Square End Fold*
*Highly conservative—any fabric*

## The Triangle Fold

Bend three corners of a pocket square into the center, and leave the remaining corner to be displayed above the pocket rim. The is a straightforward fold that is also very elegant, and is most notably associated with formal occasions. It is also a fold that works well with all materials.

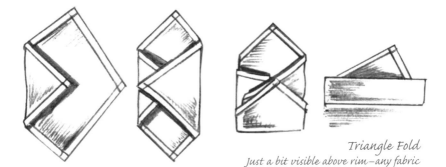

*Triangle Fold*
*Just a bit visible above rim—any fabric*

## The Crushed Fold

Make a circle with your thumb and forefinger and pull the center of the pocket square through, letting it bunch like a bouquet. Knot it loosely at the center, or fold it over and tuck into the pocket in a casual arrangement. The points should face up 1 inch above the pocket rim. This type of fold works well in silk.

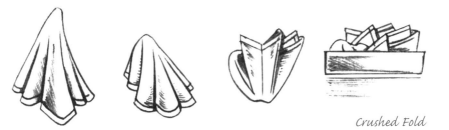

*Crushed Fold*
*Points face up one inch—best for silk*

## The Puffed Fold

Create the crushed fold, but make the knot or fold at the points instead, not at the center. Place it in the pocket exposing the puffed portion above the rim. Silk is the best material for creating this fold also.

*Puffed Fold*
*The crushed fold turned*
*upside down—best for silk*

## The Multi-Point Fold

Fold the handkerchief into a slightly uneven diagonal creating two or more points facing out from the pocket rim. When placing the fabric into the pocket, be sure the points are facing toward your man's shoulder. This will accentuate his shoulders, emphasizing his chest and upper body. This fold works best with cotton or linen.

One final note: a pocket square or handkerchief should never fall below the rim of the pocket, nor should it stand higher from the rim than 1½ inch.

*Multi-Point Fold*
*Two to four points—best for*
*cotton or linen*

# 19

# The Right Accessories

*" The only thing that separates us from the animals is our ability to accessorize."*

Olympia Dukakis

## Cuff Links

Cuff links first appeared in the 13th Century in the French court of Louis IX. It was not until the 1850s, however, with the advent of stiff cuffs on men's shirts that the cuff link came into its own. During this period it was the English who become the noted designers of these intriguing and decorative accessories for men. For most of the 20th Century, cuff links were associated with business or formal environments, but today they are commonly accepted in casual wear.

Many styles of cuff links have evolved to fit a variety of tastes and occasions. Here is a description of each and the required dexterity to help you make the best choice.

### 1 Double-Faced

These cuff links have two identical faces at either end of a short chain link. The two faces are to be displayed on the outer sides of the cuffs with the tension on the chain holding the link in place. To employ double-faced links, the faces must–one at a time–be inserted through the cuffs. This is tricky to do with one hand. (Here is where a second pair of hands can be a great help.) Popular materials used on the links faces include semi-precious stones, gold, silver, a combination of gold and silver, black onyx, and mother-of-pearl. The double-faced cuff links are considered the most fashionable.

## 2 Silk Knots

Silk knots are literally a very short silk cord tied with two tight knots at either end. Like the double- faced links they must be threaded through both the cuffs until one knot is displayed on either side thereby holding the cuff in place. Because the cord is stiff, unlike the chain on the double-faced link, they are easier to fasten with one hand. Silk knots come in a variety of solid colors, or in two color combinations. They are suitable for most occasions, but they are more casual then their double-faced brother. Because they are relatively inexpensive, yet versatile, they make nice small gift items.

## 3 Pushthroughs

These cuff links have a slightly curved metal rod in place of a connecting chain. There is a larger display face on one end and a bulb on the other which is small enough to be inserted though the holes in the cuff, but large enough once through to hold the cuffs together. Unlike the double-faced chain links, which are difficult for a man to fasten alone, pushthroughs, even more so than silk knots, can be easily managed. They are therefore another good selection for the man who lives alone.

## 4 Hinged Back

These cuff links have a larger face on one end of a rod with a small hinged bar on the other. Once the rod has been buttoned through the holes in the cuff from the outside of the cuff to the inside, the smaller bar is rotated so that it becomes perpendicular to the hole. This locks the cuff in place. The hinged back link is considered an inferior design as its moveable parts make it more susceptible to breakage.

## 5 Snap-On

In this design, the two ends of the cuff link are snapped together where they meet in the middle of the cuff. This link holds well once it has been secured, and while it can be worn for most occasions, its main problem lies with the fact that it comes in two pieces; one piece too many to lose under the bed or behind the sink.

## 6 Mother-of-Pearl

Cuff links designed in mother-of-pearl are traditionally worn with formal "white tie and tails," and with semi-formal tuxedos. Mother-of-pearl is also popular for studs, which replace buttons on a tuxedo shirt. Studs and cuff links, unlike a tie and pocket square, should always be a matched set. Antique shops are wonderful places for finding exquisite cuff links along with matching studs.

Always remember, when choosing cuff links for him, whether they are for formal or casual wear, classic is the key. Never choose a set that is overly ostentatious.

# Cuff Link Shapes

### Double Faced
*Identical faces separated by a chain link*

### Silk Knots
*Two tight knots of silk*

### Pushthroughs
*Display face at one end
with bulb at the other*

### Hinged Back
*A face at one end
with rotating hinge on the other*

### Snap-on
*Two ends snap together*

### Mother-of-pearl
*Appropriate for white tie and tails*

## The Collar Bar (or Pin)

A collar bar is a narrow silver or gold ornament which is worn under a tie. It is either pinned or attached by a spring mechanism to the two sides of a man's shirt collar in order to keep the knot of the tie prominent and the two points of the collar together and in place. It may often resemble a large safety pin and is most often worn with rounded shirt collars or with collars with long points. Since a collar bar tends to draw the collar higher on a man's neck, it is not a good choice for a man with a short neck. Also, because it is hidden for the most part, it tends to be understated in its design.

## Collar Stays

Collar stays are stiff short pieces of plastic or metal that fit into a vertical sleeve in the points of a dress-shirt collar to keep them straight and crisp. They come sewn in or removable for laundering.

*Collar Stays*

## Tie Bar (or Clip)

A tie bar (or clip) is a spring-loaded device used to fasten the front and back blades of a standard four-in-hand tie to a man's shirtfront, much in the same way as a paper clip fastens papers. Its history dates back to the Edwardian era, with a resurgence of popularity in the 1950s. It can be made of gold, silver or even enamel. It keeps a man's tie from falling into his soup, and helps the tie maintain an arch near the knot at the top. It is easily clamped onto the tie from the side in a slight downward direction, and adds a  subtle elegant touch.

*Collar Bar*

*Tie Bar*

# The Watch

The wristwatch as we know it today became popular in the 1920s. Before that time, men wore pocket watches or "fobs" stowed away in a tiny pocket of their suit vest. Today the wristwatch has largely replaced the pocket watch and, as one of his more prominent accessories, should be carefully selected for quality and how well it will go with his wardrobe (unless multiple watches can be purchased).

The appearance of a Cartier™ or Rolex™ logo on the wrist denotes superior status. If these brands are too pricey for you, a thin, nicely shaped watch with a light-colored face will also send a quality message. (It is generally considered that the thinner the face, the better the quality.) Always keep to a medium-sized face; if it is too large, it will cause premature fraying of his dress shirt cuffs. For the band, black leather is regarded as formal and conservative, while non-expandable gold, silver or stainless steel will be perceived as outspoken. If your man favors a leather band for everyday, it should be of smooth quality leather ideally in the same color as his shoes and belt. (There are many manufacturers that make fine watches in affordable styles that meet these criteria.)

Watch

If he prefers instead the convenience of an all-occasion watch, encourage him to select a well-fitting band in a combination of gold and silver which will compliment both gold and silver cuff links. For a formal tuxedo, he will have to switch to a simple, thin, small-faced watch with a plain black leather band. Gold and silver bands are not appropriate for formal wear.

*Eyeglasses*

## Eyeglasses

A man who wears glasses is perceived by some to be more intelligent and more prosperous than a man who doesn't. With this kind of effect, glass frames–as with other small but important components of his attire such as collars –must bring out his best facial features.

Here are a few things to consider when helping him to choose the correct frames:

1 A long face can be offset by choosing frames with horizontal movement.

2 A round face appears more oval if frames have strong vertical lines.

3 To lengthen the nose, look for a frame with a bridge that rests high on his nose.

4 To shorten a nose, select a pair with a bridge lower down.

5 If he has small features, choose a frame with narrow rims or no rims so as to not overpower his face.

6 Wire rim, horn rim, black or tortoise shell frames are suitable for business. Whether the frames are plastic or metal is inconsequential so long as the glasses are made well and fit his face correctly.

7 Sunglasses are one of the few necessities that also make a man look cool. Every man should buy himself a pair of fashionable sunglasses for protection as well as sex appeal. Note that sunglasses should not be worn indoors, and certainly never for business since his colleagues and clients look to the eyes to communicate sincerity, honesty, and trust. Since ultraviolet light from the sun can cause serious eye damage, see to it that he chooses sunglasses that filter out 99-100 percent of these harmful rays. The principles for selecting sunglass frames are the same as when selecting regular eyeglasses.

## Contact Information

Although good glasses lend an air of savoir-faire, contact lenses are great for improving an older man's looks, as they will take years off his age. If your companion is younger, he may like eliminating the exasperation of losing glasses. However, because glasses impart an image of authority to a younger man, he may decide to forgo contact lenses, at least in the office. I have heard of younger men with perfect vision going so far as to buy non-prescription glasses to wear during business hours.

One last thing: no matter how well his glasses look on him, if they have smears and scratches it will diminish his overall appearance. Just as it is important to keep a daily shine on his shoes, his grooming routine should include keeping the lenses and the frames clean and unblemished.

## The Briefcase

A briefcase is a man's pocket book. Like pocket books, briefcases can be expensive. If your man works in an office, encourage him to buy the best briefcase he can afford in the same color as the shoes he wears most often. A good quality briefcase will have full-grain leather inside and out, brass hardware, and a solid combination lock. If such a briefcase is out of his price range just now, a portable case made of nylon canvas for carrying his business papers will make a far better impression than one made of cheap leather.

Unlike a woman's pocketbook, a man should never carry bulky personal items in his briefcase. A briefcase is a place for business papers, not a place for storing an extra pair of socks or his lunch.

*Briefcase*

## The Pen

It is important for him to carry a pen of an excellent quality. See to it that he owns, for example, a silver or gold Mark Cross or Tiffany model. Should someone ask to borrow his pen, the quality of his choice will make the same statement as tastefully engraved business cards. If he won't splurge for himself, purchase one as a gift or suggest it to friends who need a suggestion for his birthday.

## Rings

Men should never wear more than two rings at a time. A wedding ring (should he choose to wear one) and a school ring are logical choices. Many men have a family ring of which they are extremely fond. This is an excellent alternative for the class ring. Pinkie rings are considered ostentatious and should be avoided. Suggest he have that pinkie ring slightly enlarged so he can wear it on the third finger of his right hand.

*Pen*

# The Umbrella

A not-to-be-forgotten accessory is the umbrella. Taken from the Latin word "umbraculum" meaning a shady place, this useful, often elegant item dates back to Egypt and 1200 B.C. and later became a symbol of wealth and position throughout the Orient and Africa. It finally made its way to Europe in the 16th Century and by the 1930s, with the invention of the motorcar, umbrellas had totally replaced walking sticks. Today, an umbrella that accompanies a man's purposeful stride lends him that certain air of confidence and dignity.

Umbrella

Although originally constructed of silk, umbrellas have evolved into push-button, pop-up, lightweight, tightly-woven nylon varieties with handles (found only in better shops) that are still created from one of many exotic materials including Palm (malacca) from Sumatra, rosewood from Indonesia, and birch from Sweden.

A well-made, fine-quality umbrella, purchased in either a full-length or collapsible version, can last your man a lifetime provided he doesn't misplace it. And if the mechanism should become damaged, a favorite handle can be re-used; a reputable umbrella maker will simply replace the stainless steel frame and nylon cover.

Umbrellas come in several lengths. Help him choose the length that is most comfortable for him. Remember that the darker the color of the umbrella, the more formal it becomes. Black is always a good choice, either solid or as the dominant tone in a very subtle geometric print or paisley. Black will move comfortably from business to the most formal occasion, provided that the umbrella handle is a classic crooked or right-angled design. Bright-colored umbrellas with a handle in the shape of a duck or horse's head should be carried on only casual occasions.

# 20

# Staying on Top of it All

*"Grab your coat and get your hat. Leave your worry on the doorstep. Just direct your feet to the sunny side of the street."*

*Dorothy Fields*

A man's overcoat influences the kind of impression he makes as much as–if not more than–his suit or other regular apparel. Decisions about his outer layer should not be left to chance. In fact, overcoats worn during business hours are a vital part of the total executive uniform. Fortunately, there are some conventions regarding overcoats that will help you determine the best style as well as fit for your companion's needs and budget. Here is some background that will help you purchase an overcoat that will look good for several years, making your investment a sound one.

## The Overcoat Overview

Overcoats are worn for warmth. Cold weather materials are generally heavier, weighing approximately fourteen ounces per square yard. For spring and fall, the fabrics used are a bit lighter, about twelve ounces per square yard. Overcoats often come in fabric blends so as to provide warmth with longer life.

As to styling, single-breasted overcoats generally come with notched lapels, while lapels on double-breasted coats are peaked. Both single and double-breasted overcoats will always have a single back vent.

# Wool

The best material for an overcoat is wool. Here are a few wools and wool blends that you should or, as the case may be, should not consider.

## Tweed

Tweed is a rough-textured woolen, which is both practical and warm. Harris tweed, Shetland tweed, Cheviot, Donegal, Herringbone, and Melton are all members of the tweed family. Tweed contains a high fat content, which makes each of these virtually, if not completely, water repellent– a real plus for cold, wet climates or seasons.

## Camel Hair

This brown or tan lightweight wool comes from the undercoat of the two-humped Bactrian camel found in the highlands of China. Camel hair is beautiful as well as a practical fabric for coats. It is often mixed with other wools for increased durability.

## Loden

Another light as well as very warm fabric, is loden, traditionally found in olive green. It is made from the rough wool of Austrian mountain sheep and it is naturally waterproof due to its high fat content. Loden is often blended with softer camel hair for pliability.

## Melton

This plain-weave woolen fabric with its fuzzy texture is primarily used for making heavy overcoats. It traces it roots back to the 14th Century and the hunting area of Melton Mombray in Leicestershire where British royalty traditionally wore it for their hunting parties.

## Lamb's Wool

This highly resilient wool, which is shorn from a lamb seven years of age or younger, spins and weaves beautifully, is highly elastic, and has a very gentle hand (touch).

## Cashmere

Woven from the soft undercoat of the Kashmir goat, cashmere is sensual to the touch and extremely warm. When displayed in stores, it exhibits rich, subtle tones due to its ability to accept dyes better than any other wool. Although it is very expensive, it has a reputation for not wearing well. Choose instead a cashmere/wool blend, which will provide both beauty and practicality for the long term.

## Vicuna

This rare, expensive and fragile material, which comes in tan or brownish orange, is taken from the once nearly extinct vicuna (the smallest of all camels) living high in the Andes Mountains. Because of its extremely high cost and fragility, it lacks practicality.

## Color

If he will own only one overcoat for business, it should be navy, black, or dark gray. Even a second coat should be in one of these classic colors. For casual occasions, if the budget allows, a camel hair is a tasteful choice.

## Coat Linings

The lining of an overcoat can be as beautiful and luxurious as its exterior. It is often made up in a medium- to heavy- weight satin that allows your man to slip easily in and out of it. Some satin fabrics used for lining coats are two-sided, a smooth satin side visible on the inside of the coat with a flannel textured side hidden from view. This type of fabric provides both beauty and warmth. Another lining material favored by tailors is Bemberg cuprammonium. Although this fabric is a form of rayon, and is therefore extremely durable, it also has the sensuous feel of silk.

## Overcoat Styles

There are numerous styles of overcoats that are appropriate for business wear, some lending a conservative look, others something more contemporary. There are also choices that are always dress-down. Here is a rundown of each:

## The British Warm

Originally manufactured for warmth in heavy Melton wool, this coat was designed as a uniform for British officers during World War I. Worn with a peaked cap, jodhpurs, and field boots it was both practical and handsome. Today the British Warm, with woven leather buttons instead of brass, slightly longer length, and with or without epaulets (decorations sewn or buttoned onto its shoulders), is still a handsome garment. Presently made up in other lighter-weight fabrics such as camel hair, or cavalry twill (a tightly woven, tear-resistant fabric) with a rayon or satin lining, its strong shoulders, tapered waist and slightly flared hem provide warmth and attractiveness to most men's physiques.

*The British Warm*

# The Polo Coat

This is the classic collegiate coat introduced to America in 1910 by Brooks Brothers. It is cut full, comes double- or single-breasted, and is made up in camel hair or in a cashmere and lamb's wool blend.

Most polo coats have cuffed "set-in" sleeves, but they can also come with a raglan sleeve. The set-in sleeve (which is more commonly associated with formal coats) is cut vertically at the shoulder point, like the sleeve on a suit jacket. The raglan sleeve is attached at the collar instead of at the shoulder creating the characteristic diagonal seams to beneath the arm. The beauty of the polo coat lies in its versatility. It can be worn for casual or dressy occasions and thus is an excellent choice for a young man's first business overcoat or for the man who prefers to own only one good coat. It falls below the knee, has a half belt in back, genuine horn buttons, and its patched pockets are flapped.

*The Polo Coat*

*Set in-sleeve, cut vertically at the shoulder.*

# The Chesterfield Coat

*"When a man is once in fashion, all he does is right."*

Lord Chesterfield

The Chesterfield coat, a winter overcoat, made up in cashmere or wool, is the epitome of male elegance. It is the correct coat to be worn with black tie and tails. Like the versatile polo coat, however, it is an evening as well as daytime coat.

*The Chesterfield Coat*

Its style was introduced by the British Earl of Chesterfield during the 19th Century, and continues to be recognized even today as a genuine classic. Slightly shaped with a plain back, flap pockets and a single breast welt pocket, it can be found in either a single-fly front or double-breasted version.

The darker the color the dressier the coat becomes. Fabric colors for the Chesterfield include camel, brown herringbone, dark gray, navy, or black. Its shorter lapel and collar can be constructed in the same fabric as the rest of the coat, or the upper portion of the collar can be designed with a more formal looking, contrasting black or brown velvet.

If the Chesterfield coat is worn over white tie and tails, your man must take care to see that the length of the coat is sufficient to cover the tails. At such occasions, a long white silk scarf (checked at the door) should be worn as an accessory.

## Topcoat

A topcoat differs from an overcoat in that it is not worn for warmth but in spring and summer as a finishing touch over a suit or dinner jacket. It is made up of fabric weighing twelve ounces per square yard and is shorter than an overcoat.

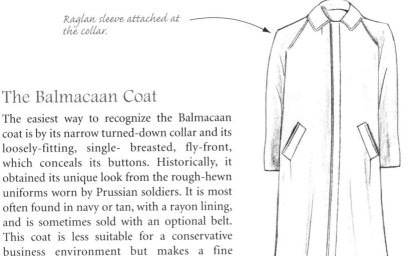

*Raglan sleeve attached at the collar.*

## The Balmacaan Coat

The easiest way to recognize the Balmacaan coat is by its narrow turned-down collar and its loosely-fitting, single- breasted, fly-front, which conceals its buttons. Historically, it obtained its unique look from the rough-hewn uniforms worn by Prussian soldiers. It is most often found in navy or tan, with a rayon lining, and is sometimes sold with an optional belt. This coat is less suitable for a conservative business environment but makes a fine impression in non-traditional lines of work.

*The Balmacaan Coat*

# The Trench Coat

Since the 1980s, the name Thomas Burberry has been synonymous with the classic raincoat commonly referred to as "the trench coat." Like the British Warm, its roots are deep in the battlefields of WWI, and it is no wonder this durable, tightly-woven gabardine cotton coat is impervious to all weather conditions. It is constructed with double thickness in back and a high storm collar for protection against the elements. In addition, it has wide lapels, storm pockets, gun flaps, shoulder epaulets, and buckled straps on its wrists, and comes either single- or double-breasted. An added advantage is that the trench coat has a button or zip-out lining, providing year-round wearability.

*The Trench Coat*

Although belt-less trench coats are sold, the most popular style has a belt. The belt is for looks but also keeps the coat tight against the body in windy weather. There are several acceptable ways to wear the belt: buckled in the back, tied at the waist in front, or buckled conventionally with the tip pushed up behind the belt and looped back under itself to hang downward. It is business-appropriate attire and is popular on chilly spring or fall days, especially when rain is forecast.

In terms of length, the classic trench coat should fall below the knees.

*"The trench coat is the only thing that has kept its head above water."*

*The Wall Street Journal*

# The Duffel Coat

The double-vented, square-tailed duffel coat is a timeless style manufactured today specifically for men's dress-down wear. It got its name from a small seaside town in Belgium, and during World War II was the trademark of British Field Marshal Bernard Montgomery. You will recognize it as a three-quarter-length coat made of a heavy tan or navy wool. The duffel coat features a yoke, an attached hood, and in lieu of buttons, peg-like wood or horn toggles, which are pushed through a hole and anchored under giant loops made of leather. This coat is traditionally worn for fall and winter weather.

## Variations on a Theme:

As you shop you will find endless variations on each of these styles. It is best not to stray too far from the classic version, however, as it ensures your man timeless design with versatility. As with a good suit, the price of a good coat can be a large part of your man's clothing budget—classics provide value over many years of wear.

*The Duffel Coat*

# Identifying Quality

In selecting outerwear always check first for a quality fabric. This can be a very enjoyable part of shopping for a man's coat. Take your time running your hand over the surface of the coat. Enjoy the luxurious, non-fattening, buttery feel of a cashmere wool blend, or similarly the rough spongy texture of a Donegal tweed. Feast your eyes as well on the depth of the fabric's color.

To further investigate the quality of the coat, take the time to do a check as follows:

· Inspect the stitching, and make sure there are no loose threads.

· See that the lining of the coat, including the sleeves, as discussed previously, is made of a medium to heavyweight satin or quality cuprammonium rayon. A trench coat with a zip-out lining should be made up in a wool and camel hair combination so as to provide both warmth and softness. You will also come across acetate taffeta used as a lining for coats. It is, however, known to fade over time and does not hold up as well.

· Check the inside of the coat also for superior workmanship. Make sure the seams are finished off with seam binding tape.

· Test all zippers. There is nothing more frustrating for your man than to struggle with a zipper every time he wears his coat.

· Avoid a coat with plastic buttons, or be sure to replace them. They have an inferior look and can break very easily. Horn buttons are best and can be recognized by their uneven color and lack of shine. Between the buttons and the coat itself, look for a small knot or plastic disk placed there as reinforcement.

## Proper Fit

Buying the correct size should be one of your main concerns when shopping for outerwear. If the coat is too small, it will look skimpy. If it is too roomy, he will resemble a clown. For a dressier coat, have your man don the sports jacket or suit that he will most likely be wearing before leaving the house for the shopping expedition.

In order to fit properly, a dress coat must have a collar that lies smoothly against his neck and rests high enough to cover his shirt collar. The correct sleeve length for a coat is at least ½ inch longer than the sleeve of his jacket. The body of the outer layer must also provide enough room for the suit or sports jacket to fit comfortably.

For a duffel coat or any other casual outer layer there is more room for experimentation. Still, consider whether he plans to wear heavy- or lighter-weight sweaters underneath when selecting a size. Again, "dressing the part" means obtaining the best possible fit even with a bulky outer garment.

## Length

One critical aspect of any overcoat style is its length. An overcoat should fall 2 to 3 inches below his knees. Shorter than that and it will throw off your man's proportions and make him look top-heavy. The one exception to this rule is a "car coat," which comes in a mid-thigh length (34 to 36 inches long). It is designed for driving and requires a minimum of bulk below the hips for increased agility. The single vent in the back of a coat should extend no further up than the bottom of his derrière both for warmth as well as for a more graceful line.

If the coat is being worn with white tie and tails, the coat will need to cover the tails, and should fall 6 to 7 inches below the knee.

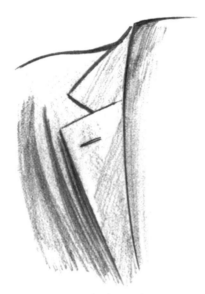

*Notched Lapel*
*Single-Breasted coat*

*Peaked Lapel*
*Double-breasted coat*

## Gloves and Scarves

Good quality men's dress gloves are most frequently made of chamois, pigskin, or leather. "Mocha," which is extremely good quality pigskin, is the most expensive leather. They can be lined with nylon, cashmere or even fur. Leather gloves, aside from looking elegant, are extremely important for a man who travels a great deal. They are the best protection from colds and flu spread by the straps on buses and subways, or public handrails. Less formal, but attractive just the same, is the knitted glove. Knitted gloves are made of wool or cashmere.

The color of a man's gloves should match his shoes. The only exception is the gray deerskin glove, which is traditionally worn with black shoes.

Quality men's scarves are made up in natural fabrics such as 100 percent wool, cashmere, lamb's wool or silk. For formal and business attire scarves should be purchased in the solid colors of white, dark blue, black, or burgundy and in traditional patterns of paisley and polka dot. A man's scarf when carefully chosen can pull together and provide the finishing touch to a perfect ensemble. All the rules for "mixing and matching" that we have already discussed in Chapter 15 apply here in choosing the right scarf for the cut and fabric of the coat.

For casual occasions, your choice of scarf will be guided mostly by his coloring. Since the scarf lies close to the face, be especially careful about how its color enhances his skin tone and the degree of contrast as covered previously. Be aware that many men find a scarf of 100 percent wool hard to tolerate, as it can give them a neck rash. Therefore, be sure to  check with him about his fabric preferences before buying.

# 21

# Cautiously Casual

*"It is possible in England to dress up by dressing down, but it's a good idea to be a duke before you try it."*

*John Russell*

During the 1950s Stanford University's brain child, Silicon Valley, the largest industrial park of Internet technology companies, began to change the rules for appropriate office wear in a way that has never been reversed. Run primarily by young entrepreneurs who hadn't been influenced by conservative business climates and who wanted to be comfortable while spending long hours at work, the high-tech companies took a "laissez faire" attitude toward dress at the office. The rest of the business world soon took note. Today, it is estimated that 90 percent of all American offices have instituted a policy of "Casual Fridays," affording its employees the luxury of dressing down the last day of the week.

## Fraudulent Fridays

Casual Fridays–or what I like to call "Fraudulent Fridays"–seem to offer a man a chance to relax and choose freely what he will wear to work that day. Don't let your man kid himself. The choice is anything but easy. He must know right from the start that Casual Friday is not synonymous with faded sweats, soiled T-shirts, rumpled or torn jeans, or sneakers. He is now required to purchase for a single day of the week a whole new wardrobe which will hopefully not destroy the entire image he has so carefully cultivated the previous four.

Casual clothes appropriate for office wear can require even more deliberation to make sure he looks professional and well put together. The objective is not only to put his various clients at ease but to retain his status among his associates, without making him look stiff and stodgy.

Here's a close look at key wardrobe items necessary for Casual Fridays, as well as social occasions requiring a relaxed but stylish look.

## The Core Jacket

As a suit is to Monday-to-Thursday attire, the Casual Friday jacket will serve as the core from which your man can select other items. This jacket should be in the business traditional colors of navy or charcoal gray, with the introduction of dark brown as a good third choice. The jacket should be of a quality fabric, have a more easy-going construction, soft lapels and display lightly padded shoulders. Excellent tailoring, as always, is still essential.

## Tried-and-True Navy Blue

The classic navy blue blazer in 10-ounce serge wool is the most popular and versatile sports jacket a man can purchase. It is the one look whether single- or double-breasted, which crosses over from social occasions to Casual Fridays without missing a beat. The navy blazer is traditionally worn with charcoal or light gray flannel trousers. At a later time, you will want to encourage him to upgrade his navy serge blazer to one in a combination of cashmere and wool for a more luxurious look.

## Trousers

To go with these less-structured jackets, he is going to need three or four pairs of trousers made of fine fabric with a good cut. Choose trousers (or slacks) that will easily coordinate in both color and texture, such as those in gray flannel, dark worsted blends, or wide-ribbed corduroys (cords) for winter and well-pressed, darker shades of khakis for summer. Trousers, when worn with a sports jacket, should never match the jacket exactly.

Casual Friday trousers should be as clean and neatly pressed as the trousers he would wear on any other business day. Corduroy and flannel trousers in shades of rich brown and beige combine especially well with tweed jackets. Most importantly, let him know that jeans are very seldom appropriate in the office unless he works at home or, as the boss of his own company, he is attempting to set a very casual standard for his employees.

## Shirts, Sweaters and Ties

An assortment of soft button-down oxford broadcloth shirts in various colors and patterns, knitted sport shirts, round or V-necked sweaters in cashmere or merino, turtlenecks and long-sleeved T-shirts should likewise be acquired for the Casual Friday ensembles. Each should be selected to coordinate with all previously selected jackets and trousers. Remember, with sweaters and pullovers, the darker their color, the dressier they are.

Casual shirts can be worn with a or without a tie. If he enjoys wearing a tie, wool, cashmere or lightweight silk ties have a rich yet relaxed look. If he prefers to go tieless, have him try tying a scarf (or ascot) with a four–in-hand knot and tucking it into the collar of his shirt for a more pulled-together look. T-shirts can also be worn beneath a V-necked sweater or a soft-collared shirt. One of my favorite looks is a merino or cashmere turtleneck worn under a sports jacket.

## Classic Casual Looks

*Button Down Oxford*

*The Navy Blazer*
*Can be single or double-breasted*

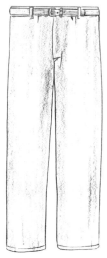

*Dress Chinos*
*Khakis*

# Casual Looks With A Sports Coat

*Button down collar with open neck*

*Scarf tied with four-in-hand knot*

*Round neck T-shirt with V-neck sweater*

*Turtleneck sweater*

## A Suit Jacket versus a Sports Jacket

Even though he may be tempted, your man should avoid substituting a suit jacket for a sports jacket. The lines of a structured suit jacket, as well as its fabric, will never adapt properly to a different pair of trousers. The buttons on a suit jacket will give him away as well since they are more polished and less rounded than those on sports jacket. The trousers from a suit, with their specific cut and formal fabric, will also conflict with a sports jacket.

## Summer Social Events

For those times when he is able to get away from work to attend summer social events, he should own at least one casual summer suit and two unstructured sports jackets in lighter fabrics and colors. Seersucker (a shirred, striped fabric most often found in a combination of white and light blue, green, yellow, or even pink) has a crisp, cool look. Although seersucker suits are a suit, in warm weather they qualify as "high end" casual attire.

If he has a light-colored summer jacket and would like to wear it for a dressier social function, suggest he combine it with a pair of darker-colored trousers. Adding the darker trousers will create a more formal look.

# Khakis and Chinos

The cloth from which khakis are made is a closely woven cotton that was originally made in Manchester, England, exported to India during the British occupation, and later again to China (hence the name "chinos" which today refers to a lighter weight khaki). Khaki was chosen by the United States military for its uniforms largely because it is durable, washable, and because of its camouflage-like color.

Khakis are the most popular leisure pants for men because they can be found in many different weights and accommodate many shirt styles and colors. Khaki can be combined, no matter what the season, with long- or short-sleeved T-shirts, sweaters, and even the traditional navy blue blazer. Khakis are commonly purchased in white (Dockers), or in various shades of beige, or olive green. Remind your man that khaki trousers should always be ironed.

## Jeans

For hanging out and even going out on weekends, nothing is as appropriate as the pervasive and always comfortable pair of jeans. Made of denim, a sturdy twill fabric first woven in Nimes, France over two hundred years ago, they take their name from the sailors of Genoa, Italy who were the first men to wear them. Jeans can be worn year round and work as well with T-shirts as they do with heavy sweaters.

Depending on the type of workplace and the preference of his boss, jeans can on occasion be appropriate for Casual Fridays but, as stated previously, caution is advised. It is always better to be a little overdressed than underdressed.

## Casual Shoes and Socks

The shoe worn on Casual Fridays or outside the office for casual social events is normally found in an earth tone rather than black. Even in casual shoes, however, there is a hierarchy of chic; the ultimate in a dress-down shoe is brown suede. A popular casual look, especially when worn with corduroy trousers, is the suede "Turf" or "Chukka" boot. When shopping, it helps to remember that the thicker the sole, the more informal the shoe.

If your man wears brown casual shoes, make sure his belt is similar in tone. The thickness of the socks must also increase with the informality of the shoe. Even socks worn with casual trousers should coordinate both in color and pattern. Follow the same rules on socks discussed in Chapter 17. The important point is that the socks must continue the line and texture of the trousers or slacks right down to the shoe.

# 22

# Puttin' On the Ritz

*"If anything is worse than your own tuxedo that doesn't fit, it's a borrowed one that doesn't fit."*

The Wall Street Journal

In no other area of men's fashion is the code so strict as in formal wear. If your man attends events requiring white tie or a tuxedo, one of you will have to be aware of the requirements for acceptable dress. Don't worry; purveyors of formal wear will be able to help you select the appropriate garments and accessories. In spite of that assistance, and because it is always helpful to understand the vocabulary associated with special attire, this chapter explains the terms you will need to know as well as the dictums of good taste for each of the various dress-up occasions.

## To Buy or to Rent

Most men dread the idea of renting a tuxedo. When they have to do it they find the styles limited, the price expensive (including all the accoutrements) and most frightful of all, the tailoring sub-standard.

A number of years ago my son, Peter, had occasion to attend his first black tie affair, a celebration dinner and dance at the Pierre Hotel after the bar mitzvah of his best friend. I took him to the rental establishment, and later regretted not being particular enough about the shop or the selection. Peter was in that in-between prepubescent stage, and wound up with a jacket that was too long, trousers that were too short, and shoes that were a size too big. He looked a little like a penguin as he headed out the door (a sweet penguin, but still a penguin).

If your man must rent, do as I did not. See to it that you choose a rental company with a reputation for superior selection and world-class tailoring.

## When Buying Is Better

When a man attends two to three black-tie affairs every year, particularly if they are business related, he should bite the bullet and buy himself a well-fitting, classic tuxedo. I guarantee that from that moment on, he will have the confidence that comes with his looking good and being appropriately attired, which will translate into his actually enjoying those formal affairs–as much as you do.

If a man purchases a classic tuxedo and doesn't gain an inordinate amount of weight, he should be able to wear that tuxedo safely without it ever going out of style. This is exactly what happened with my friend Christina's father. "At my 60th birthday party," Christina told me, "my sisters and I were looking through my wedding album when to our amusement we discovered that our dad was wearing the same tuxedo, bow tie, and cummerbund that evening as he had worn to my wedding some twenty-two years before. And he still looked dapper."

## "Black Tie Optional"

Pay attention to those little words on an invitation. When the announcement states "Black Tie Optional," if he doesn't own a tuxedo, what are his options? A good suit can suffice. It should be a well cut navy or charcoal suit paired with a crisp white dress shirt. Accents should include a conservative striped or foulard tie, a solid white linen handkerchief, a pair of well-shined black calfskin shoes, and navy or charcoal socks, matching his suit. In this ensemble, your man can rest assured that he will be admirably attired.

## "Black Tie Only"

When an invitation states "Black Tie Only," there are, unfortunately, no acceptable alternatives to the tuxedo. In fact, a man arriving in anything less then a tuxedo will most assuredly insult the host or hostess. Wearing a suit conveys that the guest does not find the affair as important as does the host. In general, it is always preferable for a man to err on the side of being over-dressed rather than under-dressed. He can always excuse himself from the party early, leaving the other guests to surmise that he had an even dressier affair to attend afterwards!

## Semi-Formal Wear–The Tuxedo

The forerunner of the tuxedo is the dinner jacket (or smoking jacket), originally designed for Britain's King Edward VII in the late 1800s to provide him with something more comfortable than "white tie" for entertaining at home (or in his case, castle). Still, it wasn't until the 1920s that this concept found its way out of private homes into more public arenas. Originally all dinner jackets were single-breasted and constructed of wool, with silk lapels.

*"Dress simply. If you wear a dinner jacket, don't wear anything else on it ... like breakfast or lunch."*

*George Burns*

Beginning in the early 1930s, for semi-formal occasions the dinner jacket evolved into the traditional tuxedo jacket and trousers that we know today.

*The Tuxedo*

# About Tuxedos

Not all tuxedos are the same. Depending on the season, type of event, or simply what looks good on your man– you will want to know what style tuxedo will work best for him. Here is information to help you become familiar with this suit, its accoutrements, as well as the time-honored rules that surround wearing this elegant outfit.

## Single or Double-Breasted

Tuxedos are categorized on the basis of the jacket, which comes in both single- and double-breasted versions. A waistcoat or a cummerbund is required with the single-breasted tuxedo, while a double-breasted tuxedo, which is always worn fully buttoned, requires neither.

## Tuxedo Lapels

There are three basic styles to choose from:

1 **"The Peaked Lapel,"** which is a holdover from the design of the original formal tailcoat. It is considered the dressiest style. With its upward sweep, it is especially effective at making a shorter man look taller.

2 **"The Shawl Lapel,"** which follows the softer lines of the 1920s dinner jacket. It is also commonly found on white summer-wear dinner jackets. Although it is still in vogue, it is considered by some to be a bit dated.

3 **"The Notched Lapel"** (or step collar) with its angular opening where the lapel meets the collar, is presently a very popular style. It is decidedly the sportiest of all of the looks.

The peaked lapel, the shawl lapel, and the notched lapel can each be faced with silk, satin, velvet or the more subtle grosgrain.

## The Traditional Year-Round Tuxedo Jacket

This jacket is constructed in midnight blue or black middleweight worsted fabric. It can therefore be worn throughout most of the year. Customarily, there are one or two buttons for closure and four buttons on the sleeve, all made of black horn or covered in fabric matching the jacket's lapel. Tuxedos look especially sharp with a white linen handkerchief tucked into their double besom chest pocket, the only type of pocket deemed sleek enough for a tuxedo.

## The Summer White Dinner Jacket

For the summer months, your man may choose to substitute his traditional blue or black worsted for a jacket in white (or off-white) made of cotton or silk.

No matter what the season or temperature, your man should never remove his tuxedo jacket in public. It diminishes the whole purpose of making an event a formal occasion.

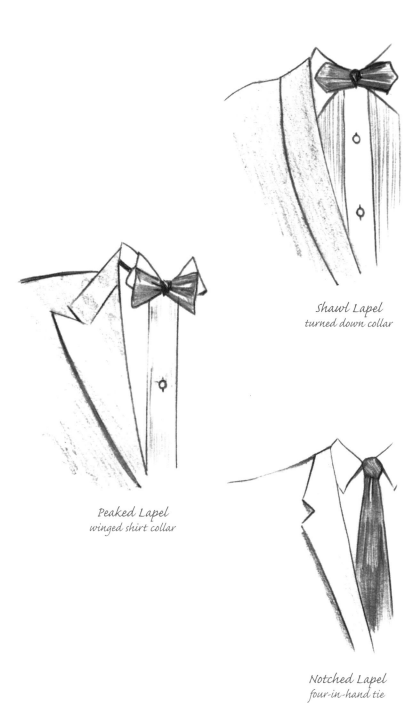

*Shawl Lapel*
*turned down collar*

*Peaked Lapel*
*winged shirt collar*

*Notched Lapel*
*four-in-hand tie*

## The Semi-Formal Tie

Unlike the formal white tie and tails, the semi-formal tuxedo can be worn with either a long black "four-in-hand" tie or a bow tie in any color, so long as they are made of the same fabric as the lapel of his jacket. A clip-on bow tie, no matter what the color or design, is not acceptable. Take the time to learn how to make a bow tie knot correctly (refer to Chapter 14 for detailed instructions). If he doesn't want to do it for himself, you will be able to do it for him.

## The Semi-Formal Dress Shirt

There are three types of shirts that are acceptable with a tuxedo:

1  A shirt with a highly starched wing collar, a bib- front and single cuffs. This type of shirt is very formal, and is worn with a single-breasted tuxedo jacket with peaked lapels, as well as white tie and tails (discussed later in this chapter).

2  A shirt with a softer, turned-down collar, a plain or vertical pleated bib front, and double turned-down cuffs.

3  A collarless shirt (or band collar) which has more recently come into fashion for men's eveningwear. Instead of having a stud at the neck, this shirt has a button.

Although staunch traditionalists might disagree on this last shirt style, all observers agree that wearing one of those overly ruffled and frilly dress shirts–so popular these days for summer weddings–is of questionable taste. Don't let him buy or rent one of these. Please!

## Cuff Links and Studs

For semi-formal wear a man may choose to wear a shirt designed with mother-of-pearl front buttons worn with cuff links or one designed to be worn with studs and matching cuff links. This matching set of cuff links and studs may be designed in gold, onyx, or mother-of-pearl; the number of studs required is determined by the height of the man, and by the number of closures found on the shirt in his size. Studs are not sold with the shirt; they must be purchased separately.

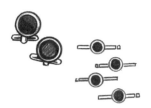

*Cuff Links and Studs*

## The Cummerbund

As mentioned earlier, a cummerbund must accompany a single-breasted tuxedo. It is a wide, pleated sash worn at the waist. (The belt being replaced by suspenders.) The pleats of the cummerbund are traditionally worn facing up in order to provide a place for stashing concert and theater tickets. Cummerbunds are most often made up in the same color and fabric as the lapels of his

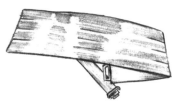

*The Cummerbund, with pleats facing up.*

jacket. Fashion purists believe that the beauty of a tuxedo lies in the stark contrast of black and white that appears throughout the ensemble. Should your man, however, desire a touch of color in his tuxedo, the cummerbund is the place to introduce it. You should remember, however, that the addition of color either in his cummerbund alone or in his matching tie and cummerbund is most successful when handled with a subtle touch.

## Tuxedo Trousers and Suspenders

The trousers of a tuxedo are always cuff-less, and are constructed of the same material as the tuxedo jacket. They also include a "single" stripe of satin or grosgrain down the outer leg (unlike the outer "double" stripe found on the trousers for white tie and tails.)

Tuxedo trousers are always worn with suspenders, not a belt. This keeps the cummerbund (or waistcoat) lying smoothly over the waistband of the trousers. The best suspenders (as mentioned in Chapter 18), even in formal wear, are made to button onto the inside of the trouser waistband. Therefore, with his tuxedo, your man should also avoid wearing clip-on suspenders, as they will cause undue bulk around his waist.

*Plain Cap-toe Oxford
patent leather or calfskin*

# "White Tie and Tails"

The dressiest formal attire for a man, and one which for economic reasons he is more likely to rent rather than to buy, is "white tie and tails." This elegant apparel, readily available at all rental shops, is worn for only the most courtly of occasions, such as opulent "after eight" evening weddings or "coming out" balls for ladies of society; and only then when a man is either a member of the wedding party or an official escort. If, however, you desire to view formal dress in all its splendor, you have only to attend a symphony concert. I openly admit I have spent many an evening with my husband (an arranger and composer) at Carnegie Hall marveling at the beauty of an entire stageful of musicians resplendent in full formal dress.

*White tie in front of the collar's wings.*

*The waistcoat.*

*Forward pleats.*

## The Morning Coat (or tailcoat)

"White tie and tails" includes a long morning coat constructed in black or gray wool. Ending slightly above the hip in front and tapering over the hip at the side, the hem of the coat extends down and around to the back of the wearer's knees with a "divided" (or vented) tail. The lapels of the collar are either satin or grosgrain.

## The Waistcoat (or vest)

Underneath the morning coat is worn a three-buttoned, single- or double-breasted waistcoat. It is shorter than the morning coat and peeks out across the stomach just enough to add another layer of formality. A tab on the waistcoat buttons to the underside of the trouser waistband in order to hold the shirt underneath it neatly in place.

## A Pique or Silk Shirt

"White tie and tails" dictates that the waistcoat is worn over a silk or stiff pique cotton shirt with a plain or bib-front, the same shirt which is worn with the most formal of tuxedo styles. This formal shirt also includes a wing, or spread detachable collar, as well as single- layered cuffs rather than the double-fold cuff found on regular dress shirts. Note that the stiffer wing collar should sit ¾ of an inch higher than the morning coat collar in the back.

## The Trousers

Formal trousers are made of the same fabric as the tailcoat, with a higher rise and slightly looser waist than usual. Like tuxedo trousers, they are held in place with suspenders. The pleats in the formal trousers are angled forward so that the wearer can put his hands into his pockets with minimum displacement to his morning coat. The trousers are also cuffless, and a pair of stripes in satin or grosgrain embellishes the outside of each leg from the waist to the ankle.

## The Bow Tie

The "white tie" and "white tie and tails" refers to the requisite butterfly or bat-wing bow tie in white that must accompany the morning coat. It should be of the same pique cotton fabric as the shirt.

*Trousers*
*with two stripes*

Position the tie in front of the shirt collar tabs. Contrary to the bow tie worn on less formal occasions, the white bow tie, susceptible to soiling, is most often sold already tied with an adjustable band that fastens at the back of the collar to minimize handling.

In formal wear, follow the same guidelines for matching cuff links and studs as with the semi-formal tuxedo.

## Those Dancing Shoes

As any woman will tell you, the effect of a lovely cocktail dress is undoubtedly compromised without the perfect shoes to go with it. The same holds true for men's eveningwear. Whether he is decked out in the exceedingly formal white tie and tails, or the semi-formal tuxedo, the right shoes on his feet are essential.

*Opera Pump*

Historically, the correct shoe for men's eveningwear was either an opera slipper or a plain cap-toe oxford lace-up shoe, both made up in black patent leather. Since the 1960s, however, a plain oxford, or even a slip-on in fine quality black calfskin, beautifully polished to a subtle sheen, has been widely accepted. I highly recommend these alternatives not only for their beauty, but because they can both be worn for so many other occasions.

## Those Silky Socks

Formal hosiery is always black, and is made of either silk or a very fine-ribbed cotton. It is important that your man's socks come up high enough to cover the calf completely. If his hosiery is very light in weight, garters should be worn to keep them from slipping down. The next time he wears his tuxedo, check out how beautifully the black silk seam of his tuxedo trousers connects to his evening shoes through the vertical ribbing of his black formal hosiery.

The glamour of a man's tuxedo cannot, in my view, be over- stated. A man never looks more handsome than he does in a well-chosen, well-tailored, and well-accessorized tuxedo.

## Synchronized Style

I believe the whole purpose of men dressing in formal or semi-formal attire is to provide the woman they are escorting with the perfect backdrop for her own eye-catching appearance. As women, we would do well to recognize this effort by men as one the highest compliments. Should you be uncertain, woman's attire for a white tie and tails affair is a long gown with sparkling accessories. For semi-formal affairs, a cocktail dress is in order in a color that won't clash with either his bow tie or his cummerbund. Dressing appropriately for all the affairs you attend together is really fun and a true celebration of all that you mean to one another.

# IV

## Preserving His Newly Acquired Assets

# 23

# Taking Care to Care

*"I don't like my hockey sticks touching other sticks, and I don't like them crossing one another, and I kind of have them hidden in the corner. I put baby powder on the ends. I think it's essentially a matter of taking care of what takes care of you."*

*Wayne Gretzky*

With the privilege of owning quality garments comes the responsibility of maintaining them through proper care. Moreover, you want to preserve your financial investment, not to mention your investment of time and effort in transforming your man through his new set of clothes! Taking care to care for good clothing is more than a matter of reading the labels. This section gives you the whys and hows that will help him form good habits.

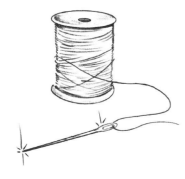

## Seeing to His Suits and Jackets

A suit is not as sturdy as it looks. The first rule of care is never to toss it carelessly over a chair and leave it there overnight. Instead, hang it properly in the closet–but not right away.

- First, remove everything in the pockets (glasses, coins, money clip, pen, handkerchief), or the weight of these small objects will eventually pull the garment out of line. Check both trouser and jacket pockets.

- Second, hang the suit on a sturdy wooden hanger on a hook located on the inside of the closet door. This will give the suit time to air out before being placed back into his closet with the rest of his clothes. If a suit is not aerated, it will retain residual odors such as perspiration or cigarette smoke, and will hold these unpleasant odors permanently. The amount of time needed for this aeration will depend how and where he spent his day. Generally, overnight is sufficient time to dispel odors. Give it the "sniff test" to be sure.

  Likewise, overcoats and sports jackets need a place to dry out (away from direct heat) after being dampened by rainy or snowy weather.

- Suits and jackets should be dusted off with a natural bristled (boar's hair) brush or a soft brass bristled brush (favored by tailors) immediately after the suit has been removed and hung on the door. This is to remove any dirt or lint acquired during the wearing. It should then be brushed again just before its next wearing in order to remove dust acquired during its stay in the closest. Over time, dirt will erode the surface of any material, causing the colors to fade and the fabric to age prematurely. It is even better if he can keep more than one type of brush on hand. Summer cottons, linens, and winter velvets want a brush with soft bristles; heavy winter woolens need medium bristles. Nappy textures such as buckskin and suede require bristles that are even coarser. Fine quality double-sided brushes are available, and these will provide him with both soft and stiff bristles.

- When finally put back into the closest, don't let the jacket or trousers become crushed by other garments. Preserve their drape and form by giving them some space to hang naturally.

## Hanging Trousers

Who can forget the scene in the film Mommie Dearest when Joan Crawford, playing the screen goddess, unceremoniously screeches at her daughter,

### *"No more wire hangers!"*

Joan Crawford may have been hysterical, but she had a point. After they are worn, trousers should be zipped up, buttoned, and hung up at full length on a separate trouser hanger (with special care taken to align the crease in both legs). Folding trousers over a wire hanger will damage the fabric where it bends, creating a permanent crease across the knee.

The best kind of apparatus for hanging trousers is the hanger that grips the trousers neatly from the waist or from the hem of the legs. The clips holding the trousers should have soft, rounded edges so as not damage the fabric or leave impressions in the material.

If one of these special hangers is not readily available, try the ingenious method used by Savile Row tailors with just a standard wooden hanger. Hold the trousers upside-down with the hanger between the legs. Then drape one leg over the hanger at the knee from one side, and then drape the other leg over the first leg from the opposite direction. Trousers hung in this way will not slip off.

Wooden hangers made from cedar, while expensive, are best. They not only provide sufficient support, they also have a very pleasant scent and offer protection from moths.

## The Savile Row Fold
for keeping those trousers on the hanger

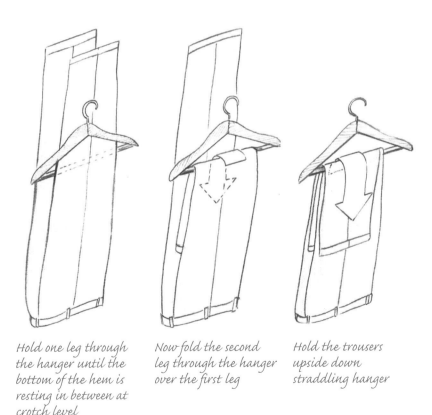

Hold one leg through the hanger until the bottom of the hem is resting in between at crotch level

Now fold the second leg through the hanger over the first leg

Hold the trousers upside down straddling hanger

# Some Pressing Issues

*"Keeping your clothes well pressed will keep you from looking hard pressed."*

*Coleman Cox*

A woman could never live without an iron, but many men do. If your man falls into this category, go out and buy one for him. While you're at it, get him an ironing board too, with a thick cushioned cover that can be removed and washed. Once he has an iron and a board, some advice on how, when and where to use them is in order. Along with ironing, provide him also with tips on steaming clothes, which can be not only clothes-saving but time-saving also.

## The Steaming Alternative

Even before getting out his iron and board, the wrinkled item should be hung in the bathroom while he is showering. After it has been fully steamed and allowed to dry, the wrinkles will probably have fallen out by themselves.

## Repeated Steaming

If he has purchased a camel hair overcoat or a cashmere sports jacket, they should be steamed on a regular basis. Camel hair and cashmere need moisture infusions to counteract the dryness caused by hot air heat in houses and apartments. Aside from a steamy shower, there are a number of hand-held steamers on the market which will do the trick. However, cashmere will also on occasion require a professional steam pressing at a reputable dry cleaner. Never use a steam iron at home on his cashmere coat as it is highly susceptible to scorching.

## Reverse and Steamed Pressing

When necessary, a suit can be safely ironed by lightly pressing it on the reverse side, or by placing a damp, clean cloth between the outside suit material and the iron. The iron should be set to the correct heat for the material being ironed. (The temperature will be indicated on the iron.) Use extreme caution as a scorch mark, once created, is impossible to remove. Ironing a suit on the right side without the protection of a pressing cloth will also produce a permanent shine. Gabardine suits are the most susceptible. Consequently, it is best to have a gabardine suit pressed lightly by a professional dry cleaner. Never try to press a gabardine suit yourself.

## Overnight Pressing

When traveling, having a suit pressed overnight, rather than having it cleaned, is the way to go. Almost every business hotel provides the service of picking up a suit at night, having it pressed, and returning it early the next morning. It is a good idea to take advantage of such a service whenever it is offered. Both the man and the suit will feel fresher for it.

## More Formal Pressing Problems

In preparing for formal occasions, never attempt to touch up the silk or rayon on his tuxedo jacket lapels as they are particularly susceptible to heat, and there is a very good chance that the tuxedo will be totally ruined. Likewise, velvet dinner jackets should never be ironed. They should be exposed instead to the steaming shower treatment.

## Pressing Trousers

Unwrinkled trousers with a freshly- ironed crease always look best, but be warned–trying to press the crease back into a pair of trousers has its own set of challenges. Except for soft, high quality wool, materials hold any crease until the next dry cleaning. For that reason, care should be taken to find the original crease in the trouser. And again, don't forget to use a pressing cloth to protect the material from scorching. On the casual side, corduroy trousers, which seldom require pressing, should be steamed on the reverse side to avoid crushing the pile.

## Ironing Shirts

Shirts can be pressed and laundered successfully at home if you follow requirements for their care. ( See the section devoted to shirts later in the chapter.)

*"I buried a lot of ironing in the backyard."*

*Phyllis Diller*

# That Favorite Sweater

Sweaters should never be hung on a hanger, wooden or otherwise, since doing so will create points at the end of each shoulder. They should not be thrown in the corner of the bedroom either. "It drives me crazy", says Sandy, a talent coordinator for a major network game show. "My boyfriend has beautiful sweaters, and I see them on the floor rolled in little balls. I am so glad that we are finally getting married so that I can pick them up and put them away."

In order to store sweaters correctly, they should be folded – both pullovers and cardigans – in a drawer or on a shelf. Soft cashmere or fine merino sweaters will not crease when they are loosely folded. It is also a good idea to rotate them in order to avoid dust settling on the top sweater.

## Washing Sweaters

His sweaters can be washed in cool or lukewarm water, with a liquid detergent for hand washing garments or mild soap flakes. In order to avoid accidentally pulling out threads during washing, turn the sweater inside out. A sweater should never be left to soak. If it is, the dirt will settle right back into the knitted fibers. When rinsing, gently squeeze, rather than wring out, the excess water. After washing, lay out the sweater on a thick towel and gently push it back into shape before allowing it to fully dry.

Hardy cotton knit sweaters are very practical as they hold up well, don't lose their shape, and seldom unravel. They do, however, become stiff when washed, as do men's knitted shirts. Dry cleaning is your best bet for these.

## Mending His Ways

*"You may turn into an archangel, a fool, or a criminal… no one will see it. But when a button is missing… everyone sees that."*

*Erich Maria Remarque*

### Sew He Knows

If he doesn't know how to sew on a button, it is a good idea to teach him. (After all, you can't always "be there.") Supply him with several needles of different sizes and thread in white, black, brown, gray, and khaki. Explain to him that a button has two sides. As elementary as that may sound, most of us at one time or another have finished sewing on a button only to discover that the part of the button facing out has a different look then all the other buttons. "Look before you sew."

When sewing on a button, it is important to sew loosely in order to leave a little space (or shank) between the button and the material. Without that extra length, the button will be extremely hard to do up and the material around the buttonhole will not lie flat. Allow slack in the thread when sewing and wind the end of the thread around the shaft before your last stitch. Also, no matter what button repair has been made, it is always a good idea to ask the cleaners to check it out and redo it if need be.

## A Stain in Time…

*"(His) business clothes are naturally attracted to staining liquids. This attraction is strongest just before an important meeting."*

*Scott Adams*

### Spotting Trouble

The most important thing to remember about stains is this; the longer a stain remains in a fabric, the harder it is to eradicate. Every man, including yours, should have access to a full-length mirror with a minimum light source of 100 watts. Not only does this assure him before leaving the house that his suit, tie, shirt and shoes go together, it also provides him with a way to spot newly acquired stains once he has returned home. (If he waits to inspect a garment before he wears it the next time, it may be too late to do anything about it.) If a garment can be taken to the cleaners within 48 hours of an accident, there is an excellent chance that the stain can be completely removed.

There are basically two categories of stains.

## 1 The Water Stain

This includes stains made by fruit juice, perspiration, blood, and alcoholic drinks–even red wine. Immediately upon discovering a water-based stain, take a clean cloth, dip it into a little cool water and pat the spot until the stain is gone. There is no point in taking a water-based stain to the cleaners, as this stain cannot be removed with cleaning solvent. (Note: This procedure applies to suits and shirts; emergency measures for tie stains is covered later in the chapter.)

## 2 The Oil-based Stain

This stain includes butter, ketchup, chocolate, salad dressing, coffee, and lipstick. An oil-based stain cannot be removed with water. Never rub a stain in an attempt to remove it, no matter whether it is water or oil-based. Rubbing will cause the dyes to run. Instead, blot the stain lightly. Resist the temptation to experiment with cleaners that may be lying around the house. It is better to have a slight stain than to wind up with a much larger and irreparable blotch that results from a botched cleaning.

Oil stains are especially troublesome as they are initially hard to spot. Only when heat, as in washing and drying, is applied to the area, will the oil stain turn yellow. Once this yellowing has occurred, the stain is impossible to remove. Oil-based stains, therefore, once spotted, must be professionally cleaned with solvents used by a dry cleaner.

Although he may be tempted to wear a favorite suit with "only one small spot" that one last time before cleaning, warn him that even a quick pressing will cause the spot to set in, making it even harder for the dry cleaner to get it out.

Be aware that many antiperspirants presently on the market contain a substance called aluminum salts. This is a corrosive agent that when mixed with perspiration leaves a highly visible stain in the form of a white circle under the arms of a silk or cotton dress shirt. When shopping for an antiperspirant, it is a good idea to take a quick look at the label to be sure you select one without this acidic substance.

If he happens to spill candle wax on a suit, sweater or shirt during a romantic evening at home, simply get out the iron and place the garment down on the ironing board with a piece of tissue paper over the spill. Now press lightly with the iron on a medium setting. The iron will heat the wax, and the tissue will absorb it. Now you can both get back to your relaxing dinner with spot out of his suit and off your minds.

At the end of every season, take – or make sure he takes – all his suits (jackets, trousers) and sweaters that have been worn to be dry-cleaned. They will then be ready for wear when the next year's season rolls around.

# The Shirt Off His Back

Laundered or Washed at Home? Dress shirts should be washed, never dry-cleaned. Having a dress shirt dry-cleaned will cause it to wilt and eventually turn gray. Ideally, a dress shirt should be washed before it is worn for the first time. During the production process chemicals are used that cause a new shirt to feel uncomfortably stiff. If you want to ensure that his shirts will come out clean when sent to a professional laundry, take an old medium bristled toothbrush and brush a little soap and warm water into the shirt's collar and cuffs at night before the shirt is thrown into the laundry bag. This minimizes the amount of time given for stains to set into the shirt fabric.

## To Starch or Not to Starch

The amount of starch in a man's shirt is really a matter of preference. A shirt that has been moderately starched tends to hold its shape better and will always look fresher than one that has not been starched at all. Note, however, that a shirt that has been heavily starched will shrink more and will wear out faster.

Heavy starching causes the threads of the fabric to become fragile and thereby break more easily. This damage is most often found in stress areas like elbows, cuffs, and around the collar. Coarser grained oxford shirts, when exposed to starch, are especially vulnerable to this erosion.

## A Professional Laundry

If his dress shirts are sent out to a professional laundry, they will be ironed with a hot pressing machine. The majority of shirts will hold up reasonably well under this treatment. Since most dry cleaners, however, will not take the time to see if a shirt label recommends a warm rather than a hot pressing, it is your responsibility to bring this to their attention. You can also request that his shirts be returned on hangers. Because protective plastic bags from the cleaner will cause white shirts to yellow over time, they should always be removed before hanging his shirts in the closet.

## Doing His Own Shirts

If he prefers to launder his dress shirts himself, here are a few tips you can pass along to him.

1 Colors and whites have to be separated. One red shirt in the bunch will create dress shirts with the unmanly color of a baby's bottom.

2 Torn shirts should not be put in the machine as the washing process will only tear them further.

3 The washer should never be overloaded. Without the room to circulate freely, his shirts will not become clean. Crowding also increases wear on the fabric.

4 Following the directions on the detergent label will give him the correct amount of soap for the size of his load. Too little, and his shirts will not be clean. Too much, and the machine can overflow, leaving a gritty residue on his shirts.

5 As was suggested when sending shirts out to a professional cleaner; in order to better clean collars and cuffs, he should apply a little extra detergent to dingy areas before washing and let it set for a few minutes.

6 The best water temperature for white shirts is hot. Colored shirts, or those marked "permanent press," should be washed in warm. Knitted shirts, because they are subject to shrinkage, should be washed in cold.

7 If bleach is required, "liquid chlorine bleach" should be used for brightening up white cotton shirts, and "oxygen bleach," a milder version, should be used on synthetics and silk.

8 Dryers, like washers, should never be overloaded. This causes stress on the dryer and on the shirt materials.

9 When drying dress shirts, do not allow them to dry on the highest setting. This will maximize shrinking. If the shirt label says "air dry only," this means the shirt is prone to shrinkage and the dryer should be set to a very low heat. Some dryers may even have a setting marked "air dry" or "air fluff."

10 He should also know that coin-operated commercial dryers become much hotter than the home variety. If he uses a laundromat, he should check his shirts regularly.

11 Shirts should also be taken out of the dryer before the drying cycle has finished and each hung immediately on a wooden hanger with the top button done. After a short time they can be ironed while still a little damp. Shirts washed and dried in this manner will need less ironing, and any ironing that is required will be easier.

12 Some men love the difference a little softness can make. Sara confesses that her husband Jake always reminded her of the princess in the children's book, *The Princess and the Pea.* "He complained about every shirt I bought him." She told me. "He was always pulling at the neck of his dress shirts, muttering to himself about how the fabric made him itch." Sara solved her problem by washing his newly acquired, unworn shirts in lukewarm water, and by adding fabric softener to the rinse water. In this way his shirts not only sustained minimal shrinkage, they never gave him a neck rash again. This is a great idea because aside from softness, adding fabric softener reduces static cling, minimizes wrinkling, and makes ironing shirts easier.

## Notes on Ironing Shirts at Home

Remember that a store- bought spray starch (or sizing), as well as water dripping from the steam iron, can cause spots on the material. Textured shirt fabrics such as seersucker, oxford cloth, twill, and pique are easier to iron then are smoother fabrics such as Sea Island or Egyptian cotton. Textured fabrics are also highly resistant to wrinkling.

# Dry Cleaning

## Spot Cleaning and Steam Pressing

Spot cleaning and/or steam pressing a suit is always preferable to having it dry cleaned. Dry cleaning, no matter how carefully it is done, dries out and breaks threads of any weave, weakening the fabric. This applies from the sportiest jacket to the dressiest tuxedo. On some materials the process will cause an unwanted sheen. A professional dry cleaning establishment will spot-clean and press a garment and nothing more, upon request. If your man takes care of his suits properly, they should not require a full dry cleaning more than three times a year, and certainly not more than every sixth wearing.

There is always some confusion over whether summer cotton trousers can be washed or should be dry cleaned instead. Dry cleaning is better. Cotton trousers will hold their shape, resist fading, and shrink less if they are dry cleaned.

If he is just starting out in his business career, and has only a limited number of business suits to rotate, help him locate a good professional dry cleaner who is convenient and offers one-hour pressing service, and/or rush overnight cleaning. Other advantages to look for include offering minor repairs and alterations, and one where the cleaning is done on the premises rather sent out to another location, increasing his chances for lost garments and forgotten requests. Even if the dry cleaner is first-rate, if your man is sending them a favorite tweed jacket or a navy blazer, he should wrap the bone or brass buttons in aluminum foil before sending it off. This will minimize damage to the buttons during the cleaning process.

After bringing home a dry-cleaned or pressed garment, as mentioned before, remove the plastic bag and give it a good shaking out. Then hang it in a cool place for a day before wearing. Woolens especially need moisture to restore their fibers, even after having been steam-pressed.

# Re-Weaving

Sometimes it just can't be helped: a cigarette ash burns a hole in his favorite jacket, or the sharp edge of a desk drawer tears the leg of his trousers. Rather than throw away a perfectly good–and perhaps cherished–piece of clothing, he has the option of having it "invisibly mended."

Re-weaving is the process by which individual threads are taken from a hidden location on a garment and are woven by hand one by one into the site of a hole or tear. The number of threads that must be transferred will depend on the type of material involved as well as the size of the hole. The best fabrics for invisible mending are heavy fabrics such as winter woolens and tweeds.

Re-weaving does have its limitations. Gabardine suits and trousers, as well as silk shirts, cannot be mended without a visible scar. Velvet jackets and corduroy casuals cannot be rewoven at all. Another issue is cost: because re-weaving is done by hand, it is very expensive. For this reason, it is best to talk with the weaver beforehand to obtain his or her advice as to whether the repair is even feasible, and to get an estimate of the cost. The time it takes to have this type of repair done is approximately three weeks. If you don't know a re-weaver in your area, a trusted dry cleaner may be able to provide a recommendation.

## Storage

Out-of-season clothing must be properly stored, mainly for the purpose of preventing the ravages of insects. An assortment of common cloth-eating monsters including moths, crickets, silverfish and carpet beetles wreak havoc on a poorly stored wardrobe. Each of these insects has a ferocious appetite and will feast on wool, flannel, gabardine, fur, cashmere, satin, and raw silk. Crickets and silverfish particularly favor men's summer knits, rayon, and fine linens. Weapons to prevent them from eating you out of home and closet include moth crystals or cedar sprays used inside the closet. If you are really lucky, you will have an entire closet lined with cedar.

Additional and convenient protection is available by storing out of season clothing in large hanging bags made of a fabric-like material (not plastic). These should be placed in an area containing some indirect light and dry, circulating air. All garments should be cleaned before being stored, as these monsters of the dark prefer gorging themselves on soiled rather than cleaned clothing. Synthetic fabrics, including polyesters and acetate, can be stored without precautions. If there is any concern that your storage area will not provide sufficient protection from damage for his out-of-season wardrobe, including his far less worn tuxedo, it is an excellent idea to store these items at a local dry cleaner until needed. This service is provided in most cleaning establishments for a standard fee.

## Fit to Be Tied

Few would dispute that the necktie holds a prominent position in a man's expression of his individuality. Unfortunately, because of its prominent position just below his chin, a tie can also express what he had for lunch or dinner.

Here are a few rules to follow to protect this beloved showpiece:

a  Both hands should be entirely clean before he puts on or removes his tie. Even the smallest amount of oil from the skin can be transferred to its highly perishable fabric. This is especially true around the area where the knot is tied repeatedly.

**b** When removing a tie, it should be loosened carefully, slipped over his head, and then, and only then, carefully untied. Yanking will only weaken or stretch the tie unfavorably.

**c** Immediately after removing a tie it should be given a quick once over in good light for any newly acquired stains. The sooner he can get it to a good dry cleaner, the better the chances are that the stain can be removed. As mentioned earlier, a stain left too long will permeate the fabric, oxidize, and become virtually impossible to remove.

**d** The same tie should never be worn two days in a row. Ties, along with suits, jackets, and shoes, need time to dry out and resume their natural state after prolonged contact with your man's body heat.

**e** Invest in tie holders with smooth edges on the hanging rods. This will protect ties from unwanted ridges. Like a pair of trousers, a tie should never be hung across a wire hanger as it will cause a permanent crease across the tie. It is also only a matter of time before the ties on a hanger will be found crumpled among his shoes on the closet floor.

**f** The only exception to this rule is the knitted tie. Knitted ties become distorted in shape when hung on any kind of rack. Therefore it is better to store them flat, or better yet, to roll them neatly, placing one in back of the other in a dresser drawer. (Begin rolling the tie from its narrow tail, toward its wider apron.) When traveling, a rolled tie can also be stored safely inside a sock.

**g** Never iron a tie. Applying direct heat will cause the fabric to become damaged, creating a shine or removing one. Also the "oh so valued" hand-rolled edges of the tie will become permanently flattened. If it is an emergency, and he simply must iron his tie, place a white cotton cloth between the tie and the iron to protect the fabric; then, after adding water to the iron, hold it just off the tie, and allow the steam to gently make contact with the material without applying any pressure. If he has the time, it is a far better idea to hang the offending tie in the bathroom while he is showering. This will allow gravity, as well as steam from the hot water, to relax any wrinkles.

**h** The delicate fabric of a tie is also prone to fading in the presence of direct sunlight. For that reason, his ties should be hung in a closet or in another dark place.

## Sudden Thrills and Spills

Every man has dealt with the dreaded accidental spill on his tie at a social gathering. Whether he or another is the culprit, suddenly every guest dips their napkin into a water glass and lunges toward him to try to rub off the newly-acquired spot. This is absolutely the wrong thing to do. If the spot is water-based, as we have discussed before, rubbing it with a wet napkin will only spread the stain and cause the dyes to run. If the stain is oil based–very possible at a social event–water and rubbing will only cause the spot to settle in permanently. Rubbing the tie with or without water will simply destroy the luster of the fabric in the area of the stain. What should be done instead?

1  Quickly, but politely, discourage any misguided do-gooders. "Thank you, but I've got it," should suffice.

2  That accomplished, take a clean white handkerchief or napkin and gently pat the stain.

3  You should then get back to the party and enjoy yourselves. Tomorrow will provide ample opportunity to bring the tie to an appropriate dry cleaner for evaluation.

4  At the dry cleaners, explain the type of stain you think it is. Specialized chemical cleaners and extensive experience is needed to do the job right. (Some cleaners specialize in ties; if your local one does not, he may be able to direct you to one who does.) Sometimes, in really serious situations, a tie may actually be taken apart, and then reassembled in order to effectively clean the affected area. Obviously, this procedure is expensive. Still, a favorite or newer quality tie may be worth the expense.

## Washing a Tie

Never attempt to wash a tie. A wide range of material is used to construct that swathe of silk or wool, and they will all shrink at varying rates even when washed in lukewarm water with gentle soap flakes. Over-the-counter stain removers are also too unpredictable to apply to a tie's fragile materials.

# Spit and Polish

*"(A man's) shoes are one of the first things that catches the eye of a woman."*

*Bruno Francois*

Wearing a pair of scuffed shoes with the soles and heels in need of repair communicates carelessness and is also bad for the shoes. What does it matter how much he paid for his Ferragamo or Bruno Malgli shoes if he fails to safeguard them?

"I live for the Ferragamo sale twice a year at Saks Fifth Avenue," Vivian gushes. "My husband Paul never cared that much about shoes until I convinced him that one pair of Ferragamos, when well cared for, could last him a lifetime. When he finally succumbed to the next sale of men's shoes, he was so proud of his new purchase that he actually took them out of their box twice in the middle of the sidewalk to show friends on the way back to our apartment. Paul also takes the time to preserve his beautiful shoes." Vivian continues, "Those Farragamos kept in their cloth bags at the top of his closet, have never felt one drop of rainwater, and have been shined meticulously before each wearing to retain their looks for the entire fifteen years that he has owned them."

As you probably know, shining shoes is not just for their looks. Proper and regular polishing in all kinds of weather sustains the leather and enhances durability. Here are the steps to take to polish his footwear investment:

1   Make sure that he has his brand new pair of shoes polished before he even wears them. This provides protection for the leather at the outset and prevents any initial scratches. Shoeshine stations are conveniently located in most towns and cities, and should make getting subsequent, regular shines easy. Shining his shoes should become a habit like brushing his teeth.

2   If he doesn't have regular access to a shoeshine station, he can still keep his shoes looking good by brushing them lightly after every wearing, and taking the trouble to clean and shine them himself as follows;

    • After every three wearings, he should don an apron and a pair of thin rubber gloves and wipe his shoes clean. (Some experts recommend saddle soap, which comes in a can and is relatively inexpensive for this initial cleaning.)

    • Then, with a dampened clean cloth or rolled up pantyhose, he should massage a good cream or wax polish into the leather. (Care should be taken to match the color of the polish with the color of the shoes.)

    • The shoes should then be laid aside to dry. If the shoes are left to dry overnight, polishing them in the morning will be easier, and their shine will be even more pronounced.

    • The final step to a brilliant shine is buffing the leather with a soft brush or polishing cloth.

Shoes must also be rotated, as in one-day-on and one-day-off. Wearing shoes for any length of time makes them damp from sweat. They will also exhibit a strong distinctive odor. Leather breathes, and if shoes are not allowed to dry out for at least a day, the perspiration that has been absorbed will cause the shoes to lose their shape.

Shoe Shine Kit

On "off" days, shoes should be kept in shoe trees (devices which hold the shoe in proper shape while allowing it to dry out more swiftly). Leather shoes will last up to three times longer with the consistent use of shoe trees than they will without. The best shoe trees are made of scented cedar wood, which absorbs perspiration more readily than plastic. He should insert shoe trees immediately upon removing his shoes at the end of the day. If he doesn't wear that pair of shoes again for a day, or weeks, or even months, shoe trees are still the way to go.

A shoe horn should also be used when pulling on shoes. They help to make the process easier, and keep the counter (the stiffening material that runs around the back part of the shoe) from being broken down by forcing the foot into the shoe.

Rain can do more damage to a pair of shoes in ten minutes than in a whole year of regular wear. Personally, I've been known to take off my shoes and walk on a wet city sidewalk rather than ruin a good pair of shoes. (I don't necessarily recommend this.) For that reason, a quality pair of shoes should never be worn if the forecast even hints of rain. If he does have the misfortune of getting caught in the rain, he should wipe off the outside of the shoes and immediately stuff them with crunched up newspaper. The newspaper will absorb the excess water from the interior. They should then be placed somewhere to dry at room temperature. After the shoes have dried for several hours, it is safe to put them in shoe trees and be allowed to dry completely. Once the shoes appear to be dry, he should wait even longer before attempting to polish them.

### Caution!
*Never make the mistake of drying out wet shoes in front of a radiator, stove or fireplace. Wet shoes dried quickly near a heat source will shrink, crack, turn up at the toes, and completely lose their shape.*

White salt stains are a real problem on leather shoes as well. The salt not only draws moisture out of the leather, it also causes cracking and staining. Once he is indoors, his shoes should be left to dry partially as previously described. Then a cloth that has been dampened with clear tepid water can be used to gently rub the surface of the shoes. (Check especially near the soles where the salt damage tends to accumulate.) After removing salt residue, shoe wax or cream can be rubbed into the leather. After waiting another hour, any extra cream or wax can be wiped away and the shoes given a normal polishing.

If he decides to spray silicone waterproofing on his leather shoes to protect them from inclement weather, he should be prepared to see the treated leather darken in color. Silicone will also cause leather to lose its luster and to crack eventually. Waterproofing is a good idea, but because of these side effects; applications should be kept to a minimum.

Minimize the  risk of rain damage by having a professional shoemaker fit good shoes with a rubber heel and having the shoes resoled regularly.

*"The sole of a man often reveals his soul."*

*Kim Johnson Gross and Jeff Stone*

## Briefly, Regarding His Briefcase

A good leather briefcase goes through a tanning process during its construction, which helps it to resist stains. If, however, he has the misfortune of having a liquid spilled directly onto his briefcase, the best thing to do is to wipe the spill away immediately with a clean absorbent cloth and then dry it completely with a soft towel (never a hair dryer, as it can cause the leather to crack). An initial stain will normally be repelled by the leather, but if left too long it will become a permanent discoloration.

## Tools of the Trade

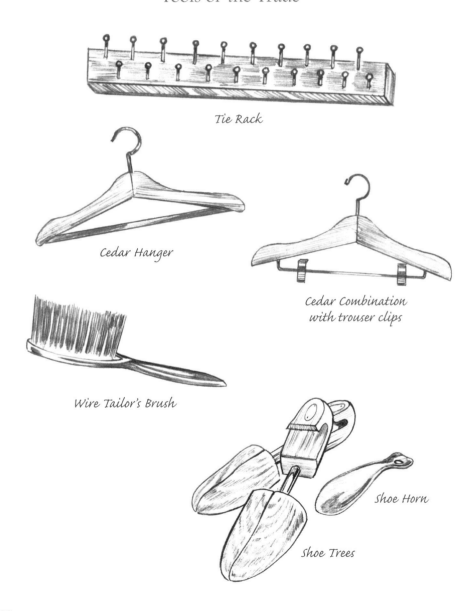

Tie Rack

Cedar Hanger

Cedar Combination
with trouser clips

Wire Tailor's Brush

Shoe Horn

Shoe Trees

In general, never use furniture polish, varnish or any kind of abrasive on the surface of a briefcase. In order to keep it looking like new, he should dust it periodically with a clean cloth. Clear wax can be used for an improved shine, but beware that any kind of wax if not completely removed will have a tendency to rub off onto his hands, his clothing, and anything else with which it comes in contact.

# V

## The Launching
## Of The New Him

# 24

# When Charting a
# Totally New Course

*" Well begun is half done."*

*Aristotle*

Most women are fortunate enough to be able to help transform their man's wardrobe gradually over a period of months or even years. Occasionally, however, there are circumstances that call for an instant plan of attack. This is especially true for the young man leaving college for a business career, or the man making an abrupt change of career or work environment. For example, my neighbor's son Jordy has spent the last four years at college, where his goal was to appear at the right time in the right room for the right class. As Jordy puts it, "Had I shown up in my underwear, no one would have noticed." But now Jordy is headed out into the corporate world with college loans to pay off, and he is going to need to be savvy about selecting a wardrobe that will allow him to fit in while not breaking the bank.

Another friend, Emily, found herself helping her husband make the adjustment from small business owner living in a remote town in Missouri to high-powered corporate executive working in a glass tower in Manhattan's financial district.

In both cases, these men were required to chart a course through the unfamiliar territory of the business wardrobe–overnight.

If your man falls into a similar category, there is a very straightforward plan that will give him a leg up in making a whole new presentation in his new job. Note that this list applies to nearly every type of industry, although Internet and tech-based businesses generally accept different, very relaxed standards of dress. Still, the new person will need to be careful in the beginning to make a good presentation and should base his ideas of what is appropriate on what the boss is wearing, not the guy in the next cubicle. For young men in very casual environments, these guidelines will still help him think through what he will need for the few inevitable occasions–either personal or professional– when he needs to be dressed up.

## Starting From Scratch–A Checklist

Build a working wardrobe with and for your man starting with these basics:

### Essential Suits

If his future, as these two examples illustrate, includes working in a big city office, especially in a law firm or a financial institution, he is going to need at least two conservative suits. The ultimate "power" solid navy blue suit should be his first purchase, followed by a suit of charcoal gray. Gray looks well with most every man's skin tones, and will make any junior executive's baby face look more mature.

These selections will also transition comfortably from daywear to an evening engagement. Choose the navy suit, the more formal of the two, for the occasional wedding or when attending a funeral. After these purchases are made, his wardrobe can be expanded to include a suit in a lighter gray or navy pinstripe (with a touch of color in the stripe).

Here are the rest of the items that he will need to form the core of his new businessman's Monday-through-Thursday wardrobe:

- **Three** solid white shirts (Sea Island or Egyptian cotton is best).

- **Two** solid blue shirts (of similar quality cotton with or without contrasting cuffs and collar).

- **Three** striped shirts.

- **Two** small checked or Tattersall shirts.

- **Six** ties selected to combine well with core suits and selected shirts.

- **Three** pairs of black shoes, either in the style of plain oxfords, buckled monks, or minimally adorned slip-ons.

- **Twelve** pairs of calf or knee length socks in black, navy or charcoal gray in either a plain or narrow ribbed weave.

- **Three** slim quality leather belts with small buckles in black, dark brown, and cordovan. A reversible belt with black on one side and brown on the other will cut this requirement to two.

- **Six** pocket squares selected with careful consideration to the colors, patterns, and textures with which they will be combined.

- **One** overcoat, which can be a British Warm, a Polo, or a Chesterfield.

- **Two** scarves of 100 percent wool, cashmere, lamb's wool, or silk, which coordinate well with the overcoat.

- **Two** pairs of gloves in chamois, pigskin, or leather lined in nylon, cashmere or fur, chosen to match his shoes.

## Necessities for Business Casual Items

In the beginning at least, he may well be putting in overtime at the office on weekends, and since "Casual Fridays" will also come around once a week, his business casual wardrobe must also be in place and ready to go.

Begin with two less-structured sports jackets in navy, charcoal or dark brown, and have on hand four coordinated pairs of trousers in flannel, wool, or corduroy. Three or four colorful oxford button-down shirts should be included to combine with ties in wool, cashmere or silk, which can then be toped with V-necked or crew necked sweaters and vests. A turtleneck sweater also combines well with a sports jacket. If the Casual Friday code in his office does not include a tie at all, colored T-shirts or patterned neck scarves will look professional and relaxed when worn under the unbuttoned collars of knitted or plain long-sleeved sport shirts. A suede lace-up shoe is an excellent choice when worn with a heavier sock. A reversible black/brown belt with a larger buckle will complete his Casual Friday picture.

# "But the Other Guys…"

Your man may come home and report that other men at the office are wearing rumpled khakis and an old button-down shirt with frayed collars on Casual Fridays. While this may be true, probably not all his colleagues are interpreting the term "dress-down" as liberally.  In any event, how a man dresses at work strongly reflects his attitude about his job, so being pulled together is important. How to present oneself in relation to others at work will be a matter of personal discretion since being too well dressed may be socially uncomfortable and non-productive. However, my belief is that  tasteful, thoughtful attire is never out of place and the kind of impression that is made by looking well groomed may very well reap benefits for him in the long run.

Once your man has purchased these core pieces, you can use all the guidelines in previous chapters to fill out his business and casual wardrobe.

# From Structured to Laid Back

If your man is leaving the highly charged competitive world of big city business for a long-dreamed-of second career in a different line of work, he is also going to have to make major adjustments to his wardrobe from formal to business casual. In this situation, his mode of dress will have to convey to his co-workers a sense of style and confidence, while at the same time maintaining his awareness of the more low-key feel of his new work environment. Don't rule out the role of the jacket, as jackets can be laid-back yet lend authority. This look may be a real asset when a person is new to an area.

## Essential Elements

His core wardrobe must now include three less-structured sports jackets as in one navy wool or gabardine blazer, a brown tweed jacket and a slightly dressier medium gray checked sports jacket. A zippered Super 100 percent wool cardigan sweater in a neutral gray or brown can also be purchased as a substitute for one of his jackets. If he is relocating from a winter environment to a summer one, his jacket choices should of course be made in lighter-weight fabrics and in lighter colors. Quality fabrics as well as good tailoring are still important.

A half dozen trousers should be chosen in colors and textures that will complement his jackets. The fabrics should include gray flannels, lighter worsted blends, wide- ribbed corduroys, and freshly-ironed khakis.

He will need to add the following items to his core pieces in order to complete his transition to a more relaxed, but well put together look:

- **Five** Oxford button-down broadcloth shirts in assorted colors including plaids and Tattersalls.

- **Five** knitted or plain cotton sport shirts with soft collars.

- **Four** short-sleeved contrasting colored T-shirts, which can be worn under open collars.

- **Four** ties in a mixture of dark solids, wool or cashmere, as well as lighter-weight, patterned silk ties (depending on the season).

- **Five** sweaters or vests either turtle-necked, V-necked, or crew-necked to go over broadcloth shirts or to be worn under sports jackets.

- **Three** pairs of substantial shoes with thicker soles, a suede lace-up shoe, and a quality leather slip-on, are all very practical and extremely good looking.

- **Nine** patterned or plain heavier pairs of socks to balance out his more substantial shoes.

- **Two** heavier belts in leather, suede or canvas in similar tones as his shoes.

- **One** overcoat, either a Trench or a Duffel coat.

- **Two** 100 percent wool, lambskin, or cashmere scarves in solid colors or in traditional checks.

- **Two** pairs of gloves in heavy weight leather, lined in cashmere, wool or fur. Knitted wool and cashmere gloves are also appropriate.

In spite of the fact that your man is now working in a more relaxed working environment, he will still on occasion, even in a small village or rural setting, be attending formal affairs. His darker business suits, classic white broadcloth shirts, pure silk ties, and plain black oxford shoes should be kept cleaned and in good order for these events.

# Helping Him When You Are Not Available

Your man may travel for business, or due to your own schedule you may not always be available for a clothing consultation when he is getting ready to leave the house. To help maintain his "together" look in your absence–at least until he is used to his new way of dressing–I have included two customizable charts in this section. One is for suits and more formal wear, and the other for casual wear, both business and personal. They can be used as a roadmap to mixing-and-matching suits (as well as sports jackets and trousers) with their best combination of shirts, ties, pocket squares, socks, shoes, and belts. The time it takes to fill in these handy reference charts is well worth what it will provide in the way of efficiency and peace-of-mind for both of you. I recommend that you start with the more formal suit chart, and once completed, move on to the casual wear, since each chart will encompass a distinctly different set of clothing.

## Special Consideration

These roadmaps will also be of great help to the man who suffers from color blindness. Color blindness is twenty-five times more common among men than it is among women. (One in twelve men are affected by it either partially or completely.) The difficulty can range from distinguishing similar colors, to extreme cases where recognizing only degrees of black, white, and gray are possible. Based on numbers and letters, the chart frees him from having to identify his clothes by their color alone.

# Creating the Fail-Proof Roadmap

When you are ready to create his roadmap for suits and more formal wear, begin as follows:

1 Take all his suits shirts, ties, pocket squares, socks, shoes and belts, and lay them out on a bed.

2 Starting with his suits, iron on a small label in an inconspicuous place, such as underneath the manufacturer's label or inside the back of the collar. (Labels used for children's clothing for summer camp will work well.) Mark each label with a capital letter, starting with A, and continue through the alphabet. (The pen you use must be labeled as having "permanent ink," otherwise your markings will disappear during future washing and laundering.)

3 Now do the same with all of his shirts, but this time use numbers, starting with the number 1.

4 Next, do the same thing on his ties, again using numbers.

5 Now do the same numbering with his handkerchiefs and pocket-squares.

6 Take the suit marked with an A and determine all of the shirts that can go with it. Fill in the proper squares on the chart indicating the numbers on the two or three shirts that will look the best.

7 Go through all the ties, and check how they complement the selected shirts and suits. Mark their numbers on the chart. You should now have two or three really good combinations of shirt and tie from which he can choose for the suit marked A.

8 Now select a pocket square (if he likes to wear one) that will best go with each of these two or three combinations, and mark their numbers in the chart as well.

9 Socks, which are also labeled with a number, will obviously have to be sewn on.

10 Shoes can likewise be marked with a number on the inside of the heel in the same location as their size.

11 Belts can be marked inside except in the case of a reversible belt–in which case the belt can be worn on either side depending on the color of the shoes or trousers.

12 Now move on to the next suit, which will be marked with the letter B and repeat the process of identifying the best shirt, tie, and so on.

When filling in the chart for his casual clothing, you will have the additional consideration of selecting the appropriate trousers to best coordinate with each sports jacket. Don't forget, as mentioned previously, you will have to be concerned with not only how the trousers match the sports jacket, but also how the trousers will coordinate with the shirt and tie alone when the jacket has been removed.

When the charts have been completed, hang them up on the back of his closet door or on the wall of the closet itself so he can get accustomed to the system. The charts will also double as excellent packing guides, and you should make some extra copies–one for him to take with him when traveling, and one for you to take when you go shopping for him. Using this numbering system, you will immediately notice any gaps in his wardrobe. And don't forget to update the chart with any new acquisitions!

# Your Man's Business Chart

| Suit | Shirt | Tie | Pocket Square | Socks | Shoes | Belt | Notes |
|------|-------|-----|---------------|-------|-------|------|-------|
|      |       |     |               |       |       |      |       |
|      |       |     |               |       |       |      |       |
|      |       |     |               |       |       |      |       |
|      |       |     |               |       |       |      |       |
|      |       |     |               |       |       |      |       |

# Your Man's Business Chart (Extra)

| Suit | Shirt | Tie | Pocket Square | Socks | Shoes | Belt | Notes |
|------|-------|-----|---------------|-------|-------|------|-------|
|      |       |     |               |       |       |      |       |
|      |       |     |               |       |       |      |       |
|      |       |     |               |       |       |      |       |
|      |       |     |               |       |       |      |       |
|      |       |     |               |       |       |      |       |

# Your Man's Casual Chart

| Jacket | Trousers | Shirt | Tie | Pocket Square | Socks | Shoes | Belt | Notes |
|--------|----------|-------|-----|---------------|-------|-------|------|-------|
|        |          |       |     |               |       |       |      |       |
|        |          |       |     |               |       |       |      |       |
|        |          |       |     |               |       |       |      |       |
|        |          |       |     |               |       |       |      |       |

# Your Man's Casual Chart (Extra)

| Jacket | Trousers | Shirt | Tie | Pocket Square | Socks | Shoes | Belt | Notes |
|--------|----------|-------|-----|---------------|-------|-------|------|-------|
|        |          |       |     |               |       |       |      |       |
|        |          |       |     |               |       |       |      |       |
|        |          |       |     |               |       |       |      |       |
|        |          |       |     |               |       |       |      |       |

# 25

# That Lovin' Feelin'

In this day of image- and health-consciousness, with many men spending their free time lifting weights and jogging, it could be that the new way to a man's heart is through his wardrobe. In other words, the wise woman will think about ways to express her interest and support through clothing, so that he feels confident about himself in any and all social situations.

No, he may not like to shop – few men do. So a smart woman like you, who has sought out information on classic menswear, endears herself by expressing candid and well-informed opinions about how he looks. With your knowledge and love, you can become an indispensable and a trusted confidante.

But there is a payoff for you, too. By sharing your newly- acquired knowledge, he not only gets to be the man he always knew he was, you get the man you always knew he could be!

And that is truly a lovin' feelin' all around.

**Apron** *(tie) Also known as the "front blade", the wide end of the standard four-in-hand necktie.*

**Argyle** *The often-colorful diamond plaid pattern used frequently on wool knitted socks or sweaters.*

**Ascot** *A type of tie worn on formal occasions. The ascot has identical square ends worn crossed over and held in place with a stick pin.*

**Balmoral Oxford** *The more formal version of the oxford shoe, featuring a closed throat lacing.*

**Brogueing** *A pattern of small holes or "punchings" of different sizes that ornament a man's shoe.*

**Back Blade** *The "tail" or more narrow end of the standard four-in-hand necktie.*

**Balmacaan Coat** *The single-breasted overcoat with a narrow turned down collar, loosely fitted silhouette, raglan sleeves, and fly-front.*

**Bar Tacks** *A large stitch made with heavy thread at the back end of the front and back blades of a tie to secure the two edges of fabric where they meet in the middle.*

**Barrel Cuff** *The most common form of cuff found on a man's dress shirt. The barrel cuff is fastened by a small button and buttonhole.*

**Bat Wing** *A bow tie, narrower than the butterfly, which also answers to the name of the "club" bow tie.*

**Bellows Pocket** *An expandable pocket that stands out from the jacket itself. It is often referred to as a "safari pocket."*

**Besom Pocket** *A pocket which is set into the jacket itself. Topstitching along the opening reinforces its narrow edge.*

**Bib-Front** *A style of shirt appropriate for formal wear.*

**Blazer** *The most versatile of all men's sport coats since it can be worn for so many occasions throughout the year depending on its fabric. The most popular color for a traditional blazer is navy blue, including brass buttons. Blazers can be single- or double-breasted.*

**Bluchers** *Another name for the "Derby" oxford shoe with open throat lacing. It is a less formal shoe than the Balmoral.*

**Boat Shoe** *Often referred to as the "deck shoe" or the "topsider," it is a slip-on shoe made of well-oiled, water-resistant leather.*

**Braces** *A British term for suspenders.*

**Break** *The amount of "dip" or "shiver" created about 4 inches above the hem of the trouser, caused by the material relaxing on the top of the shoe.*

**British Warm** *(coat) An outer coat worn primarily for warmth, and most often made up in Melton wool, camel hair, or cavalry twill.*

**Broadcloth** *A closely-woven fabric with a soft, subtle shine used in making men's shirts.*

**Butterfly** *The most popular style of bow tie that flares from the center knot to vertical straight ends curved slightly at the top and bottom. It resembles a butterfly.*

**Button-Down Collar** *The points of this collar attach to the shirt with small white buttons. It has a soft comfortable look, and is most often found on casual broadcloth shirts.*

**Cable** *(socks) An overlapping, chain-like, raised pattern found on casual knits, such as weekend socks and sweaters.*

**Cavalry Twill** *A durable cotton, wool, or man-made fiber, with a diagonal cord weave, used often for casual trousers, jackets and coats. Standard colors for cavalry twill are olive, tobacco, or beige.*

**Car Coat** *A three-quarter-length wool coat designed to make sitting and sliding out of an automobile more comfortable.*

**Cashmere** *A beautiful and costly fabric made from the undercoat of goats that roam the mountains of Kashmir, Tibet, and Mongolia.*

**Chalk Stripe** *A fabric pattern characterized by soft stripes approximately ⅛ inch apart that run along the warp (vertical) threads of a suit. Considered semi-conservative.*

**Change Pocket** *A small flapped pocket most often found on custom-made British suits. Located just above the hip pocket, it is used for holding change, tokens, or tickets. It is also known as a "ticket" or "cash pocket."*

**Cheat Pocket** *A slit on a jacket or trousers that is actually a false pocket. It is added for looks without adding bulk.*

**Chest Pocket** *Located on the left side of the jacket, the chest pocket is slanted toward the shoulder and is used as a receptacle for a pocket square. Also known as the "welt pocket."*

**Chesterfield Coat** *A winter coat (either single- or double-breasted) generally made up in cashmere or wool, which goes easily from day wear to formal evening events.*

**Cheviot Tweed** *A fishbone pattern woven from the wool of sheep found in the Cheviot Hills between England and Scotland. It is characterized by its rugged, nappy, lustrous sheen.*

**Chinos Trousers** *Similar to khakis and designed exclusively for casual wear. For wear in the warmer months, chinos are constructed in polished cotton or poplin.*

**Chukka Boot** *Another name for the "turf boot." It is an ankle boot with two- eyelets, which is most often unlined and can be constructed in either calfskin or suede. It is considered casual.*

**Clock Pattern** *(socks) A subtle linear decoration found on the outside of a dressy sock.*

**Club Tie** *A tie with a repetitive pattern of emblems associated with a specific type of activity, such as sailboats, golf tees, or tennis rackets.*

**Collar Bar/Collar Pins** *Accessories used to hold the two ends of a collar and tie in place.*

**Collar Stays** *Short stiff pieces of plastic or metal that fit vertically into or are sewn into the points of a dress shirt collar to help maintain crisp corners.*

**Cool Wool** *Another name for "worsteds." Worsteds are smoother, stronger and more tightly woven than woolens.*

**Cordovan** *Durable non-porous leather used for shoes and belts that is made from the inner portion of the hindquarters of a horse.*

**Counter** *Reinforcement that runs inside and around the back of a shoe to help maintain its shape through the repeated sliding in and out of the foot.*

**Crepe** *A wool material with a bumpy feel and a crinkly appearance, used most often in warm-weather suits.*

**Donegal Tweed** *A tweed with flecks of color woven throughout the material.*

**Duffel Coat** *A three-quarter-length coat for weekend wear made of heavy wool with a yoke, hood and toggles in place of buttons.*

**Egyptian Cotton** *Along with Sea Island cotton, the finest grade of cotton used in men's shirts.*

**Fabric Loop** *A loop of fabric sewn just above the bar tack at the back of a tie used for guiding and holding the tail in place.*

**Fitter** *The person who takes a man's measurements for the construction of a custom-made suit, but does not follow through on the actual cutting and sewing of the garment.*

**Flannel** *A material found most often in chalk stripe suits, flannel comes in various weights and can be worn throughout most of the year.*

**Flap Pocket** *The most common style of pocket, which is constructed inside the coat. Only a flap of material covering the opening is visible from the outside.*

**Flat Front** *A trouser front without any pleats.*

**Forward Pleat** *A trouser pleat with the opening of the pleat facing the fly-front of the trousers.*

**Foulard** *(tie) A pattern of repeated geometric shapes used in making neckties and pocket squares.*

**Four-In-Hand Tie** *Another name for the typical necktie, named for the resemblance of its widening shape to the gathering of reins for four horses in the driver's hand.*

**French Calf** *A highly-prized leather for the construction of men's shoes, it can be recognized by its smooth feel and matte shine.*

**French Cuffs** *A deep cuff found on dress shirts, the French cuff folds back on itself and must be fastened with a cuff link.*

**French Tipping** *A term used when the inside of a tie is of the same fabric as the front side. This is an indication of superior quality.*

**Full-Brogue Oxford** *Also referred to as a "wingtip," it has decorations on the toe in the shape of a bird with outstretched wings with further decoration running from the front of the shoe to the heel.*

**Fusing** *A method of sealing the outer and inner layers of a jacket or coat by the application of heat, pressure and a special bonding agent.*

**Gabardine** *A soft, tightly-woven fabric with strength as well as body, it is virtually water- and soil-resistant and is most often found in solid colors.*

**Gauntlet Buttons** *Small buttons located on the placket of a dress shirt sleeve which hold the opening together.*

**Glen Plaid** *A black and white box-pattern usually made up from a rough- quality tweed with a very tight weave.*

**Gorge Line** *The widest part of a man's jacket lapel.*

**Grosgrain** *Rayon or silk, woven very tightly and, in men's wear, closely associated with tuxedo lapels and cummerbunds.*

**Gusset** *A triangular piece of fabric sewn between the curved hems of the front and back of a shirt for reinforcement.*

**Hacking Pocket** *An angled flap pocket most often found on British-made suits and sporty suit jackets.*

**Half-Windsor Knot** *A medium-sized knot used for a tie that is popular with men of average size and build.*

**Hand** *The quality of a material recognized by its feel.*

**Harris Tweed** *A tweed known for its rich warm colors and its herringbone pattern.*

**Herringbone** *A twill with a weave resembling an upside-down and right- side-up capital V.*

**Houndstooth** *A pattern resulting from the braiding of four white threads with four black threads, which resembles a dog's tooth.*

**Inseam** *In trousers, the measurement of a pants leg from the crotch to the inside of the leg hem.*

**Interlining** *(tie) The pre-shrunk layer inside a tie running its entire length, ensuring that it hangs properly, repels wrinkles, and is easier to tie.*

**Inverted Pleat** *A trouser pleat where the material comes together in the center to form an interior pleat.*

**Khakis** *Casual trousers, made from a durable and long-wearing cotton twill, which can be worn comfortably any time of the year.*

**Left Dress/Right Dress** *Referring to the leg of the trouser on which a man carries his sexual organs. Most men dress left.*

**Linen** *A material made from the flaxen plant. "Irish linen" is a tight, softer and lighter-weight variety; while "Italian linen" is rougher with a less- predictable weave.*

**Madras** *Woven cotton material originally made in Madras, India which has a pattern of either checks or stripes in varying colors designed to bleed one into the other during washing.*

**Medallion Brogue Oxford** *A plain oxford shoe where only the toe cap has been decorated.*

**Melton** *A heavy woolen material with a short, nappy surface, used most often for men's winter coats.*

**Merino Wool** *The highest quality "Super wool" used in men's attire.*

**Microfiber** *A strong polyester fabric which has the property of maintaining both body warmth and coolness as desired.*

**Mocha** *An extremely fine-quality pigskin most often used for making quality gloves.*

**Mohair** *A soft shiny material made from the hair of the Angora goat.*

**Monk Shoe** *A shoe style characterized by a broad tongue and a buckled leather strap which lies across the vamp of the shoe.*

**Multi-Point Fold** *A handkerchief folded in such a way as to create two or more points facing out from the pocket's rim.*

**Notched Lapels** *A lapel with a wide-angled opening at the point where the lapel meets the collar, this style is found mainly on single-breasted jackets and coats.*

**Oxford Cloth** *A plain-weave or basket-weave cotton often used to make the classic Brooks Brothers shirt with a button-down collar. "Royal Oxford" is its best grade.*

**Paisley** *A pattern of elongated, curved shapes and intricate swirls. It is a very popular pattern for ties and pocket squares.*

**Patch Pocket** *A pocket constructed with a piece of fabric sewn directly to the outside of the garment found mostly on sports jackets.*

**Patent Leather** *A material from which men's formal evening shoes are constructed, it is created by a process of exposing leather to extreme heat, polishing it, and then applying several coats of lacquer.*

**Peaked Lapels** *Lapels that point upward and leave only minimal space between the lapel and the collar.*

**Pinstripe** *Fabric with a very fine vertical stripe, each set about ¹⁄₁₆ of an inch apart, pinstripe suits are considered to be the most popular and highly conservative pattern in men's apparel.*

**Placket** *The "front placket" is the double strip of fabric down the center of the dress shirt where the buttons are located. The sleeve placket is the location of the tiny buttons securing the sleeve opening.*

**Pocket Square** *A decorative handkerchief in silk, silk-blend or cashmere, used for ornamentation only in a jacket breast pocket.*

**Polo Coat** *The most versatile men's coat. Cut full, it comes either single- or double-breasted and is generally made up in camel hair or a cashmere/lambs wool blend. Also known as the classic "collegiate" coat.*

**Puffed Fold** *A reversed crushed fold used with pocket squares where the puffed portion is exposed above the rim.*

**Punchings** *This is another name for decorative "brogueing" on shoes.*

**Raglan Sleeve** *A fuller-cut sleeve attached at the collar and extending down diagonally to the armhole. Often found on men's overcoats.*

**Regimental Stripe** *A pattern of diagonals used on ties, the multi-striped ties with a solid background originally bore the colors associated with specific regiments, worn by their members. Today, many color variations exist.*

**Reverse Pleat** *A trouser pleat with the opening facing outward toward the pocket of the trousers.*

**Re-Weaving** *A process by which a fabric can be "invisibly mended" by taking threads from an inconspicuous place on the garment and weaving them by hand to repair the damaged area.*

**Rise** *In trousers, the amount of room between the top of the waistband to the bottom of the crotch.*

**Sea Island Cotton** *Along with Egyptian cotton, the finest grades of cotton used for making men's shirts.*

**Seersucker** *A summer-weight material with a crinkled texture most often found in combinations of white alternating with either blue, gray, green, yellow and sometimes pink.*

**Semi-Brogue Oxford** *A shoe with a straight-line decoration on the toe cap which may or may not have decoration over all or a part of the rest of the shoe.*

**Set-In Sleeve** *A sleeve cut vertically at the shoulder, as is found on a traditional suit jacket.*

**Sharkskin** *A dressy worsted twill fabric generally found in darker shades with lighter highlights giving it a "salt and pepper" look. This pattern is also known as "pick and pick."*

**Shetland Tweed** *A member of the textured tweed family which comes most often in stripes and plaids.*

**Shoe Horn** *An instrument made of metal, horn, or wood which holds the counter of the shoe in place while the foot is being slipped in.*

**Silk Knot** *Tight knots of colored silk thread used as cuff links.*

**Slip Knot** *This is another name for the "four-in-hand" knot which is the simplest knot to tie and therefore the most popular.*

**Slipstitch** *A type of stitch used in tie construction, to allow for natural stretching of a tie with wear.*

**Snap-On** *A type of cuff link that is snapped together in the middle of the French cuff.*

**Spectator Shoes** *A two-toned oxford shoe with either semi- or full- brogueing.*

**Spread Collar** *A standard style of collar that is found with points of many heights and with varying degrees of openness, thus suitable for a large number of men. It is often referred to as a "cut-a-way" collar.*

**Square-End Fold** *This is another name for the "television fold" used with pocket squares.*

**Straight Point Collar** *With its points set close together and its clean lines, this collar ranks as the most popular with men. Its versatility takes it from daytime to evening.*

**Studs** *Fasteners used to hold together a formal dress shirt in lieu of buttons, studs must be purchased separately from the shirt, and should be worn with matching cuff links.*

**Super Wool** *The indication for a better-quality, narrower-width fiber wool.*

**Synthetics** *A name referring to man-made fibers. Some examples include nylon, rayon, acetate, and polyester. Synthetic blends refers to the mixing of certain wools with synthetic materials, which are considered high- quality textiles.*

**Tail** *The 'back blade" or narrow end of the tie which rests against a man's chest behind the apron.*

**Tailor** *The craftsman who takes the measurement for a custom-made suit from the fitter and then cuts the pattern and sews the final garment.*

**Tartan** *One of many cross-checked plaids. For centuries, each tartan was associated with a specific Scottish clan.*

**Tattersall** *Colored horizontal and vertical lines creating squares of different sizes across a solid background.*

**Thistle** *A bow tie which extends straight in either direction from its center knot, it is the narrowest of all bow ties.*

**Ticket Pocket** *A very small pocket located just above the hip pocket, usually on a custom-made suit jacket. Also known as the "change pocket."*

**Tie Clip** *A spring-loaded device used to fasten the front and back blades of the tie to the shirt front.*

**Top-Sider** *Another name for the boat shoe.*

**Trench Coat** *The classic belted, double-breasted raincoat with epaulets made famous by Thomas Burberry.*

**Triangle Fold** *A pocket square or handkerchief fold which leaves one corner of the square exposed above the rim of the pocket.*

**Turf Boot** *Another name for the "chukka boot."*

**Tweed** *A term used when referring to a large group of rough-grained woolens made up of yarns containing many and varied colors. Included in the twill family.*

**Twill** *A sturdy, raised rib-pattern resulting from the weaving of horizontal and vertical threads of a material on a diagonal.*

**University Tie** *A tie with only two broad stripes of equal width running diagonally across it, with no background color.*

**Velvet** *A silk, rayon, nylon, or cotton fabric with a short, dense, shiny pile on one side and a plain, dull surface on the other. It is most often used in the making of men's jackets which can go for casual to highly formal, depending on the material used.*

**Vent** *A vertical slit in a man's jacket or coat that permits ease of movement and access to pockets.*

**Vicuna** *An extremely soft, warm, and very expensive fabric made form the fleece of the South American llama native to the Andes Mountains.*

**Wale** *The rib running on the surface of a material such as corduroy or poplin. A wide wale is considered to be less dressy than a narrow wale.*

**Waistcoat** *Another name for a vest.*

**Weejum** *This is another name for the classic slip-on-shoe, the "penny-loafer."*

**Welted Shoe** *A shoe with a narrow strip of leather approximately 2 feet long, ⅛ of an inch thick, and ¾ of an inch wide all around the edge of the sole which provides the supporting structure for holding the sole, the insole and the "upper" portion of the shoe together.*

**"White Tie and Tails"** *The term used to denote formal dress, which may also be abbreviated to "white tie."*

**Windowpane** *Pattern used in suits and jackets that takes the form of a large check with vertical oblong shapes.*

**Wing-Tip Shoe** *A shoe with a toe cap decoration resembling a bird with outstretched wings. Further decoration or brogueing may extend from the cap to the heel. Also known as "full-brogue" oxfords.*

**Yoke** *The section of a shirt that lies on top of the shoulders, attached by a horizontal seam across the front as well as the back of the shirt.*

# Index

# Selected Bibliography

*These following books have proved of great inspiration and service to me in gaining a comprehensive overview of each of the subjects included in this book. If I have whetted your appetite to learn even more, I strongly urge you to seek out and enjoy these books, written by many of the acknowledged giants in the world of men's fashion.*

*– B.D.M.*

Amies, Hardy. *The Englishman's Suit: A personal view of its history, its place in the world today, its future, and the accessories, which support it.* Quartet Books, 1994.

Bixler, Susan. *Professional Presence: The Total Program for Gaining That Extra Edge in Business by America's Top Corporate Image Consultant.* Perigee Books, 1991.

Boorstein, Steve. *The Ultimate Guide to Shopping & Caring for Clothing.* Boutique Books, 2002.

Boston, Lloyd. *Make Over Your Man: The Woman's Guide to Dressing Any Man in Her Life.* Broadway Books, 2002.

Boyer, Bruce G. *Elegance: A Guide to Quality in Menswear.* Norton, 1985.

———— *Eminently Suitable: the Elements of Style in Business Attire.* Norton, 1990.

Bridges, John and Bryan Curtis. *A Gentleman Gets Dressed Up: What to Wear. When to Wear It. How to Wear It.* Rutledge Hill Press, 2003

Calasibetta, Charlotte Mankey. *Fairchild's Dictionary of Fashion.* Fairchild Publications, 1975.

Cabrera, Roberto, and Patricia Flaherty Meyers. *Classic Tailoring Techniques: A Construction Guide for Men's Wear.* Fairchild Publications 1984.

Chaille, Francois. *The Book of Ties.* Flammarion, 1994.

Cochran, Andrew G. *Tying the Knot: The Sharp Dresser's Guide to Ties and Handkerchiefs.* Abbottsford, 1997.

Flusser, Alan. *Dressing the Man: Mastering The Art of Permanent Fashion.* HarperCollins, 2002.

———— *Making the Man: The Insiders Guide to Buying and Wearing Men's Clothes.* Wallaby, 1981.

———— *Style and the Man: How and Where to Buy Fine Men's Clothes.* HarperCollins, 1996.

Gross, Kim Johnson and Jeff Stone. Michael Solomon & David Bashaw. *Dress Smart Men: Wardrobes That Win in the New Workplace.* Warner, 2002.

Gross, Kim Johnson and Jeff Stone. Michael Solomon & James Wojcik. *Shirt and Tie.* Knopf, 1993.

Hollander, Anne L. *Sex and Suits: The Evolution of Modern Dress.* Knopf, 1994.

Jackson, Carol. *Color for Men.* Random House, 1984.

Karlen, Josh and Christopher Sulavik. *The Indispensable Guide to Men's Clothing.* Tatra Press, 1999.

Karpinski, Kenneth. *Mistakes Men Make That Women Hate.* Capital Books, 2003.

Keers, Paul. *A Gentleman's Wardrobe: Classic Clothes and the Modern Man.* Harmony Books, 1987.

Lurie, Alison. *The Language of Clothes.* Henry Holt and Company, 1981.

Lenius, Oscar. *A Well-Dressed Gentleman's Pocket Guide.* Prion Books Limited, 1998.

Omelianuk, Scott and Ted Allan. Esquire's Things a Man Should Know About Style. Berkley, 1999.

Piras, Claudia and Bernhard Roetzel. *365 Style and Fashion Tips for Men.* DuMont monte Verlag, 2002.

Schoeffler, O.E. *Esquire's Encyclopedia of 20th Century Men's Fashions.* McGraw-Hill, 1973.

Vass, Laszlo, and Magda Monar. *Handmade Shoes for Men.* Konemann, 1999.

# Quick Order Form

**Mail Orders**
Betsy Durkin Matthes
Peter's Pride Publishing
PO Box 3026, Shelter Island Heights
New York 11965-3026

**Please send the following book.** I understand that I may return it for a full refund for any reason, no questions asked.

*Name* _____

*Address* _____

*City* _____ *State* _____ *Zip* _____

*Telephone (day)* _____ *(evening)* _____

*email* _____

*Quantity* _____

**Sales Tax: New York State residents only**
Please add ___.___% as appropriate for your county or city.

**US Postal Service Shipping costs**
Regular Mail        $5.00
Priority 2-3 days   $7.00
Canada: Air Mail    $8.00

**Payment**
Send check or money order; all orders shipped when check clears.

**To order using your credit card**
Go to http://www.PetersPridePublishing.com
Click on "To Order" from Amazon.com

**Signed copies available from the Author**
Clearly print name of recipient _____